D0669406

SMALL CHANGES:

BIG IMPACT

MAXIMIZE YOUR PRESENCE AND LEVERAGE THE POWER OF YOUR PERSONAL BRAND

NADIA BILCHIK & KAT COLE

Greater Impact Communication
Atlanta, GA   *Johannesburg, SA*

This book is a work of nonfiction. Unless otherwise noted, the author and the publisher make no explicit guarantees as to the accuracy of the information contained in this book and in some cases, names of people and places have been altered to protect their privacy.

© *2013 by Nadia Bilchik & Kat Cole*

All rights reserved, including the right to reproduce this book or any portions thereof in any form whatsoever.

small Changes: BIG IMPACT: Maximize Your Presence and Leverage the Power of Your Personal Brand

ISBN: 978-0-9885013-0-0

ISBN: 978-1-6248802-9-2 eBook

Printed in the United States of America

For Nelson Mandela:

Who by changing one country,
impacted the entire world.

.

TABLE OF CONTENTS

A NOTE FROM THE AUTHORS

Throughout the book, "we" refers to the two of us, Nadia and Kat.

Five years ago, we met at a panel discussion on leadership and realized that although we had very different career paths, we shared a common spirit and philosophy. We also had the desire to assist others to develop greater confidence, poise, and influence in all areas of their lives. Whether it's the many workshops and training events that we have authored or led, or our personal experiences in life and in business, we share common lessons that have fueled our collaborative efforts to train, develop and mentor others.

After every training event over the years, we have discussed the need to provide a tool that supplements the event and provides a reference and guide beyond the workshop. Very often, we give a 45-minute keynote address, and while we are thrilled at the positive impact that can have, it leaves so much unsaid. This book provides detailed experiences and information that we often have to leave out in our brief appearances. It is now yours to be read at your leisure.

Although we provide insights and recommendations on maximizing your presence and impact, there are few things more influential than authenticity. As you read each chapter, we suggest that you internalize the concepts and tips and apply them in a way that works for you individually.

We want you to remember at all times that it is important for you to celebrate who you are: in fact, as Oscar Wilde has said: "You may as well like yourself, because everyone else is taken."

Be you... the real you... and, whatever your position, highlight your strengths while leveraging the techniques we share, to elevate your personal presence in business and in life!

This book is a culmination of many workshops, coaching endeavors, and speeches that we've worked on together. The situations we mention are real; the people are real. In some cases, to protect their privacy, we have changed the name. At your disposal are the findings, techniques, and mindsets from the best of both of our experiences.

INTRODUCTION

Where were you ten years ago? In business and in life, how far have you traveled? Do you feel like you have accomplished your goals and made progress? Or do you feel that there is little distance between the current you and the you that first started out on a particular career path?

Ten years ago, Nadia Bilchik was a new arrival in Atlanta, Georgia. She had left behind a prime time anchor position and training career eight thousand miles away, in Johannesburg, South Africa, and faced the prospect of starting all over again from scratch, unknown and knowing absolutely no one.

Ten years ago, Kat Cole was a hardworking restaurant employee and a student in Jacksonville, Florida, with goals of furthering her education and helping support her and her family's personal goals.

Today, Nadia is the founder and chief executive of Greater Impact Communication, providing training, consulting, and keynote addresses to the Coca-Cola Company, Turner Broadcasting, CNN, Cartoon Network, Delta, The Home Depot, ESPN, Kaiser Permanente, and

Saks Fifth Avenue, among others. She has also produced and anchored feature programs for CNN International, and currently reports for *Morning Passport* on CNN Weekends.

Kat has turned her detour into the hospitality industry into a highly successful career: Over the course of just nine years, Kat has advanced from her first hostess job to becoming a vice president of a billion-dollar international hospitality company, and currently she's the president of Cinnabon, the global baked goods chain and franchise, at the age of 33. Kat, who recently graduated with an Executive MBA, is also a highly sought-after speaker for a wide range of companies, universities, media outlets and industry organizations, including AT&T and Sanofi Aventis and has appeared on HLN, CBS, Fox and CNBC among others.

What are the qualities that enabled Nadia, an immigrant to the United States, to reach for and attain the American Dream? Kat was one of many equally qualified candidates at each point of her career, but she was the one who always advanced to the top. What are the qualities that have enabled them to be so successful in such challenging and competitive industries?

There are questions that probably get asked a thousand times a day: In a work environment that is frequently filled to capacity with highly skilled and productive individuals, how do you develop the special qualities, the kind of Polish, Poise and Influence that will make you stand out above others? What can you do that will give yourself an edge over often equally impressive and competent individuals? What techniques and qualities can you use to ensure that you not only get and keep the job you desire, but also are recognized and poised to take advantage of additional opportunities?

Nadia and Kat explore the answers to these questions, and show you the *small Changes* you can make that will give your Personal Presence the *BIGGEST IMPACT* that is possible.

* * *

The task is going to be much easier than you think. It's likely you already know much of what you are going to read in this book, so while we don't promise you huge revelations, we do promise you a series of **B.L.O's**, otherwise known as Blinding Lights of the Obvious. These are ideas and practices that you have probably already learned, but given the hectic nature of all of our lives, you may have forgotten them along the way. Often all it takes to begin to Maximize Your Personal Presence is simple self-awareness and greater consciousness of the way you communicate. And we are honored that you are joining us on what we know will be an extremely productive journey for you.

Now, it is normal to assume that the individual who stands out within a pool of equally qualified candidates is the person who is "naturally blessed" with good looks, charisma, and charm. Indeed, that can be the case; there are people who have an innate, compelling presence without knowing how or why. But as we will demonstrate, the process is less magical than you may think. In fact, there are specific characteristics and behaviors that hiring professionals and executives consistently name as the differentiators between otherwise identically and technically qualified individuals.

Whether you are just entering the job market, or are a seasoned executive looking to make a professional transition, or someone who simply wants to have a great impact and advantage in the workplace, these differentiators are the common denominators of those who "show up, speak up, and move up" in any professional environment. They are the qualities that add up to what we call your "personal brand" – the culmination of everything you say and do that contributes to the perception of who you are and what you are really about.

Your ability to persuade and influence is largely based on the perception others have of your personal brand, a perception that is created moment by moment, step-by-step, by everything you say and do over time. However, in the whirlwind of activity, we often forget to engage these qualities that enhance our professional presence. What a pity to not take advantage of and use all the techniques and best practices at your disposal to elevate your personal and professional impact!

The good news is that we have identified the key strategies and personal qualities that can give you the edge you need. Moreover, they are strategies and approaches that you can learn and put into practice in order to elevate your professional impact, stand out from the pack, and accelerate your career.

Conversely, and of equal importance, there are many common traits among those individuals who are unlikely to find or be offered new opportunities. You may be unconsciously or inadvertently ignoring the opportunities to enhance your personal brand and professional presence, or not implementing tools and techniques at your disposal.

We call the factors that diminish opportunity "derailers" because they literally are capable of throwing your career trajectory off track. And it is vitally important to become more aware of what you do that may act to block your ability to move forward, and to learn to mitigate those behaviors and attitudes – or better yet, avoid them altogether. If you think of your personal brand as an equation, there are behaviors that add value, and there are those that subtract. Derailers are exclusively those characteristics or behaviors that subtract and lessen the overall impact of your professional presence.

Is your impact and influence as powerful, persuasive, and compelling as it could be to take advantage of the opportunities that lie before you? Do you inadvertently sabotage yourself through a lack of self-awareness? We will help you recognize what it takes to have a powerful presence and show you how to develop, implement, and enhance these winning skills and qualities.

We spend a lot of time in our seminars reminding people why they have value, and teaching them to articulate and embrace their own unique qualities and skills. Just as we take teams through all of the elements of the "personal brand enhancement process" we will give you techniques to practice the personal strategies that we ourselves use successfully in our daily lives and careers.

If you have only a hammer and nails there are only so many things you can accomplish as a builder, but if you have access to the many tools available to enhance your ability to craft and build, the opportunities are endless. Our intention is to broaden your awareness of such tools as they relate to enhancing your personal impact, and we challenge you to put them in place to grow your career!

There are many *small Changes* you can make to have the *BIGGEST IMPACT*. We have narrowed them down to the following essential elements:

1. THE FOUNDATION OF PROFESSIONAL PRESENCE & LEVERAGING THE POWER OF YOUR PERSONAL BRAND

Learn and leverage the Equation of the Three A's:

- Awareness
- Accountability
- Attitude

2. PHYSICAL PRESENCE

The verbal and nonverbal qualities that communicate who you are when you interact "in person."

Learn how to give yourself an edge by always being physically present in any situation utilizing the components of Executive Presence. This includes delivering professional presentations, communicating with poise, and dressing and carrying yourself like a world class professional.

3. INTERPERSONAL PRESENCE

Minimize and avoid common derailers or sub-tractors: Learn more about your personality type and how your personal style affects how you interact with others in various situations.

4. SOCIAL PRESENCE

Develop and expand relationships inside and outside of your company and industry. Learn to effectively connect by building meaningful, reciprocal relationships. Learn from experts in the field to master all of the most effective relationship building strategies.

5. VIRTUAL PRESENCE

Build your personal and professional community through virtual interactions like those on the phone, e-mail, and web-based social media. This includes a section on how to "put it all in writing".

We will share with you real world insights and specific advice both from our own experience and from others who have lived by these principles to grow their own careers. These are individuals who have successfully served as leaders and coaches to help others maximize their potential for success and gain competitive advantage in the workplace.

Every journey has its obstacles, and we have certainly made and continue to make our share of mistakes. However, they have served as valuable lessons. Regardless of the derailers we all inevitably face, with our guidance you will soon be more poised to deal with them with grace, and accomplish success in a most enjoyable and almost effortless way.

If you're reading this and finding yourself thinking, "I can't do all of that," don't freak out! Even if you just do a few things better tomorrow than you do today, if you just make some small adjustments, you are increasing your chances of success.

No one is suggesting that you must do all of these things to be successful, but we believe if you take advantage of some of the techniques to enhance your personal brand and professional presence, you will be that much more successful, more often, more quickly, and more easily than many others.

CHAPTER 1

FOUNDATIONS AND BEYOND: The small things that Enhance Your Professional Presence and give you BIGGER IMPACT in any Situation

We take it as a given that you are good at your job; maintaining your skills and performance level are essentials, especially in uncertain economic times. Our focus, therefore, is on those extra elements, both verbal and nonverbal, that will help to differentiate you from other equally qualified, proficient individuals. These are the qualities that add up to the kind of Professional Presence that gives you a competitive advantage.

How do we define Professional Presence? It is a combination of polish and poise, the sum of the qualities you project that communicates confidence and competence. It draws on many factors, including how you carry yourself, and how you communicate and interact with others – both in person and virtually.

Essentially, we are talking about the combination of your image and your interpersonal skills, because these are the qualities that will help you stand out. If you look at people whose careers have accelerated, their advantage does not come from their performance alone; rather it comes down to how they project themselves, and how they relate to other people – be they colleagues, superiors, or potential customers. These are the people who have constructed their careers and success on the four cornerstones of Emotional Intelligence: drive, self-awareness, empathy, and acute social skills.

These are the skill sets that we teach in our Presence seminars, and the more we witness them in action, the more we see how vital they are for career success.

Central to this are what we call the three A's of Self-Improvement:

- **Attitude**
- **Accountability**
- **Awareness**

ATTITUDE IS EVERYTHING...

Ask any manager what they consider to be one of the most important traits of a valuable employee, and you will find that "having a positive attitude" gets a very high ranking in their professional order of importance. People do not respond well to individuals who project gloom, and make it clear they are not open to doing anything that is outside of their job description or comfort zone.

Example: Christine H. who manages a busy and high-pressure hospital department, says she values employees who are "not complainers", the kind of employees who approach their jobs with a positive "can do" attitude. In fact, she values, and is likely to promote, individuals who show by their attitude that they understand the pressures on her, and go out of their way to help.

"There are certain people on your staff who know how busy and overwhelmed you are. When you ask them to do something, they are going to say 'Sure', and 'No problem', because you wouldn't be asking them if you didn't really need this," Christine says. "The one who says that, and does it with a smile, is the one you naturally want to give opportunities to."

Having a positive, "What can I do to make your life easier?" attitude can also help open the door to opportunity. We often cite the example of an individual, Natashia L., who passed up on the chance to meet and impress a senior executive at her company, by taking the attitude "It's not my job." In this case, Natashia refused to pick up the senior executive at the airport on a Friday afternoon, on the grounds that the traffic was going to be terrible, and the task did not fall under her job description. In contrast, Chris R., the employee who cheerfully agreed to act as a driver, had the opportunity to meet with and impress an executive who several months later was in a position to propose and support Chris' application for a promotion. You never know what small interaction can have a *BIG IMPACT* on your life and career.

Even better, go one step further. Come to work early, stay late, and strive to finish that project early. In addition, you will really make strides if, within the bounds of what's possible, you think of innovative things to do within your work environment without being asked to do so. "Take it one more step on your own," Christine recommends. "But this is where your inter-personal skills come in, because you need to be sensitive to how busy your boss is. Don't send in volumes of material you weren't asked for, but have the information when the time comes. You want to be the reliable, solid one who keeps your boss informed. But don't overdo it. Be proactive, but not pushy."

ACCOUNTABILITY ADDS MORE...

Unless you are a high-ranking officer in the military, or a monarch, you can't dictate how people respond to you. One deceptively simple principle is that the only way you can get the kinds of results that you are seeking – be it a promotion, a sale, or a new job – is to alter the view of others in such a way that it impacts what they think of you or how they act.

We, and the organizations that we work for, must take responsibility for ourselves and be our own agents of change and success. If not me, who? If not now, when? This is a favorite phrase of ours that expresses the simplest form of accountability. If we truly want change, we have to look to ourselves to create it.

While many others have played a role in our careers and successes in life, we never underestimate the impact that our own determination to be accountable for our outcomes has had in our journey.

BE ACCOUNTABLE TO YOURSELF...

Always keep in mind that how you feel about yourself – your internal attitude of personal accountability and presence – is projected onto your external persona. If you lack confidence and a feeling of self-worth, it is reflected in how you approach people, and even by how you hold yourself.

At the times when you are feeling down, positive self-talk can help you feel better about yourself, and thus project a more attractive image. This in turn can help to set up a self-reinforcing loop, because your colleagues are then much more likely to respond positively to you. It may sound simplistic, but let us assure you that many of the most successful people in the world do it, some naturally and others through practice and coaching.

Try it now. Say to yourself: "I've gotten to where I am because of my abilities. I have a unique story. I'm good, smart, and extremely capable. There are many reasons why I am successful in my career." Say it every day, every time you're alone. Write it down, and put it on your desktop. You'll be surprised at how effective positive self-talk can be!

THE VITAL A OF SELF-AWARENESS...

Some individuals are acutely aware of themselves – the kind of attitude they project, and how they relate to others. And frankly some people are clueless, and it constantly works against them, because the kinds of social skills that a self-aware individual develops are a vital element of effective professional presence. This is the case in a range of work environments.

Example: John B., who has a PhD in Operations Research, was considered one of the brightest and most productive members of his company's strategic planning division. But something was holding him back. It was only when we had a chance to observe him in a meeting that the reason emerged: John could not disguise his boredom. His arrogant body language told the other members of his group that he thought he was brilliant, and they did not have anything of much value to contribute. Fortunately, John was receptive to our observation, and in fact, he was pleasantly surprised to realize that many of his colleagues had important insights and contributions to make. This recognition helped both enhance John's career, and the success of the projects he was working on.

KNOW HOW YOU'RE PERCEIVED

Kat faced a similar challenge with a coworker who frequently complained about being passed over for promotions to several open positions in the company. Jane H., who worked as a receptionist, felt strongly that she had the technical expertise to take on a more challenging assignment, but she appeared to have little awareness of how to take advantage of her very visible position. Both the way she dressed, which was at the most casual end of the attire that was acceptable for the workplace, and the nature of her interactions with her coworkers, which tended toward the social as opposed to the professional, formed a barrier to promotion. Although there was never any question about her ability to do her current job, Jane did nothing to display that she would fit in culturally to a higher role.

Kat urged Jane to take responsibility for the way she wanted to be perceived. That meant she needed to take steps to see herself through the perspective of others, to own the situation by approaching the person who was hiring for the position she wanted, and to solve this issue by modifying the nature of her interactions with her coworkers. Unfortunately, Jane did not follow Kat's advice. Her pattern of friendly social chats at her desk continued and, as a result, she missed the opportunity for a big promotion.

It is so important to make a conscious effort to understand how you are perceived. Even a *small Change* can have a *BIG IMPACT* on your career. Raising the level of your self-awareness is one of the most effective steps you can take. We use a variety of ways to elicit feedback, ranging from innocent eavesdropping and outright asking, to written feedback. In a simple but impactful example, Kat recalls how she learned about her own annoying speech tic by overhearing a restroom conversation during a large company workshop that she thought was going perfectly well. That was when she heard a participant complain that she kept on saying "you know" over and over. Although she felt mildly embarrassed to hear the news, Kat also appreciated the feedback, and made a conscious effort to eliminate the "you knows" from her repertoire.

Only when you are aware of your style, your derailers, and your strengths, can you embrace the good, tone down the bad, and work on the ugly – the essential tasks of Emotional Intelligence and effective self-improvement.

You do not need to go through years of introspection and therapy to become more self-aware. There is a range of simple personality profiling tests you can take (we'll recommend a few later); or you can have someone videotape your presentations, meetings, or speeches. Ask a friend to give you honest and unedited feedback. All of this will help you become more informed of all the elements – good, bad, and ugly – that make up "you".

BALANCE, THE TOTAL PACKAGE...

We want to make it clear that while we are emphasizing the importance of your image, it is essential that you strive for a balance that works for you in your situation. Charm alone is not going to get you ahead if you don't also focus on doing your job effectively. Conversely, you can be brilliant at your job, but you will undermine the way you are perceived by colleagues, peers, and potential clients if you do not project the persona of an open, accomplished, and articulate person as often as possible.

A sales associate we have worked with has "all the poise and polish in the world." Unfortunately, she is so focused on her image that she has neglected the nuts and bolts of her job, and that inconsistency undermines her. Essentially, she wants all of the recognition without doing the necessary work, and she hasn't fooled anyone.

In a contrasting example, Nadia worked with an individual who, while highly effective at her job, was not doing herself justice in the image department. Tessa P. was a highly skilled and talented graphic artist, who regularly came to work in faded jeans, a prominent hoop nose ring, and old t-shirts, despite the implicitly more formal dress code at work. Her attitude was, "I can dress any way I want...after all, I'm an artist!"

Tessa was considered a valuable employee, so even a nose ring was not going to get her fired, but her appearance undermined her chances for the promotion she desperately wanted. It wasn't that she couldn't perform her role with this appearance, but it was difficult for the organization's leadership to envision her as a department head or executive.

We're not saying this is right or wrong, but it is a business reality that you are at an advantage if your superiors can envision you at the next level, and see you as consistent with the image they want to project on their leadership team. It's fine to be true to yourself, but it is also important to be realistic about the impact this could have on potential opportunities.

After consulting with Nadia, Tessa realized that on an unconscious level, she was acting like a rebellious teenager. However, once she came to agree that the only person she was hurting was herself, Tessa accepted the necessity of working on her image. She began to dress more appropriately for work while still keeping her creative individuality. She made the simple transition to a nose stud, added a black blazer, and wore more tailored jeans. She found to her surprise that her reward was also a promotion that included a much more "adult" salary!

EVERYTHING COMMUNICATES ...

To summarize: You have to deliver, but what makes you exceptional and differentiates you is how you handle conflict, articulate ideas, and project an image that communicates confidence, credibility, and authority. Conversely, individuals who focus purely on image and exposure, and neglect consistency of performance, are equally self-destructive.

The Accountability Principle emphasizes that it is people's experience of your actions in their totality that transforms their beliefs. And it is only by transforming people's beliefs that we can determine their actions and impact the results. That is why a consistency of excellence is so important.

In the whirlwind of our hectic lives, we often forget how critical some of the small things really are. Think of these attributes as tools in your toolbox. Most people have these tools, but they forget to sharpen and use them. Now is the time for you to use every tool at your disposal – the total sum of skills that will add up to your Professional Presence that will give you a *BIGGER IMPACT* in every situation.

The *small Changes* in setting the right foundation are:

- Know that how people experience you affects how they treat you

- Remember to deliver what you promise

- Adopt a giving attitude

- Consciously understand that *EVERY-THING* communicates

The *BIG IMPACT*: You will exude a level of confidence and reliability that will attract the right people to you who can greatly accelerate the progress of your career.

CHAPTER 2

GET OUT IN FRONT: How small Changes in Presentation Skills can have a BIG IMPACT on your Personal Brand

There is no question that your ability to articulate and present yourself in a public arena with clarity, confidence, and charisma is critical for your career success. Throughout our careers and business ventures we have seen many talented individuals sabotage themselves: They don't speak up in meetings, and they don't take the opportunity to make their points in a public forum and showcase their strengths.

Presentations are among your most important opportunities to make an impression, stand out, and enhance your personal brand. Often, promotions, advancement, and winning new business are based on how a person presents him- or herself publicly. Recruiters also pay attention, in some cases to the extent of hiring trained evaluators to assess a candidate's public speaking and communication skills.

Many leaders are defined by their ability to articulate their message and points of view effectively in a group. People who have used our presentation skills often return and say they are more comfortable speaking up and therefore being seen as far more capable – even though their technical expertise has not changed. The work you are doing daily may contribute to your reputation, but when you stand up and present an idea, that can be a great opportunity to showcase your strengths. Some people are naturally gifted speakers, and you may not see yourself as one of those, but every one of us can be better, and incrementally more effective than we are right now.

THE GREAT INHIBITORS

The first, and most common inhibitor is fear. If you had the choice of spending the day in a roomful of snakes, or giving a presentation, which would you choose? If you went for the snakes, you are not alone. According to Dr. Timothy Sharp, a clinical psychologist and founder of the Happiness Institute, a significant number of people are often more afraid of public speaking than they are of even dying.

Understandably, the first issue is TOTAL PANIC. If you are too nervous to put yourself out in front, you aren't going to be able to take advantage of all of the opportunities that could come your way. Fear not! What you are about to read has changed the lives of numerous people we have coached over the years.

The best antidote to nerves is to develop a POSITIVE EMOTIONAL MEMORY DATABASE in your own mind. First, think of three experiences you have had over the last 10 years that have been validating for you; three moments where you achieved something, were complimented, or overcame some difficulty. Remember those moments of triumph and reflect on how you felt at the time. Recalling positive past experiences and literally visualizing them, before speaking up in a meeting, or giving a presentation, is a powerful antidote to nerves.

The second thing that inhibits us is the perception that we must be perfect, the best, in order to take the risk. "I'm afraid of making a fool of myself," says one such petrified individual, "I'm afraid that I'll forget what I wanted to say, or that I won't be able to hold the audience's attention."

Remember this: The goal is not perfection (unless you are a speaker by trade, and even professional speakers don't need perfection); the goal is effective communication, connecting with your audience...and constant improvement.

Think of presentations as opportunities rather than burdens. There are simple strategies and techniques you can use to become an impressive communicator and a relaxed public speaker. Both of us speak regularly in front of small and large audiences, and we have learned key components of effective, powerful, and career enhancing presentations. In this chapter, we share tips and techniques we use ourselves, and that you can in turn use to polish various facets of your communication and public speaking skills. These include, but are not limited to, dealing with nervousness, improving the content of your presentation, enhancing your nonverbal presence, and adding life and energy to your delivery skills.

So, how do great leaders, actors, and politicians do it? Essentially, they have learned how to be **H-E-A-R-D**:

H – Hook your audience
E – Evidence: get the facts
A – Anecdotes: tell stories
R – Reel In: recap and relate
D – Delivery skills: The Power of How

HOOK: *HOW TO GRAB THE ATTENTION OF YOUR AUDIENCE*

In order to develop the most effective hook and immediately engage the audience, you need to ask yourself the following questions:

- Who is my audience, and what is the purpose of my presentation?

- What is their experience?

- Do they know me?

- What do I want from them? – A sale? Their votes? More cooperation and teamwork?

- What are the main points I want to make?

The bottom line of kicking off an effective presentation is understanding what you want your audience **THINKING, FEELING, AND DOING**.

Example:

- What kind of evidence or detail can you provide to support the position you are taking?

- Do you have visual support material like a PowerPoint that you want to use?

- Are your visual aids easy to read from a distance, and is their meaning clear?

Work on your "hook". You need to grab your audience within the first few seconds with a question, compelling statement, or interesting fact.

Learning HOW to HOOK your audience is going to be one of your greatest takeaways from our coaching. If you learn to do this masterfully, you will immediately be at an advantage every time you give a presentation. This technique can be learned quickly, but you must be prepared to be creative.

You need to ask yourself the following: *"What question can I ask this audience that my presentation answers?"*

Example: If I were trying to persuade my store associates to sell complements or accessories to an item, I could ask, *"Have you* *ever bought supplies for a home improvement project, and when you got home you realized you had forgotten to buy drop cloths? That happened to me last week. It was so frustrating. Well, that is exactly how our customers feel when we forget to recommend all the incidentals they need with their purchase."*

Another example was convincing a group of middle school children to become more sensitive to people less fortunate than themselves.

The hook was, *"What did you think about on your way to school today? How many of you thought about homework, school lunch, or a party on the weekend?"*

Nadia then added, *"That's what life should be like, right? But it isn't so for Jamimah Udguiambani. Jamimah is your age and she takes care of her three younger brothers, because both of her parents and also her aunts and uncles have died of HIV AIDS. Today we will look at what a problem HIV AIDS is throughout the world, how to appreciate what you have, and what we can do to make her life a little easier."* The group was enthralled, and it was a great way to kick off a heavy subject by making it relevant to a young audience.

Never start with *"I'm here today to talk about..."* That's a total snoozer!

Always ask yourself: *"What do I want my audience Thinking, Feeling, and Doing (TFD) as a result of my time here?"* Remind yourself that your presentation needs to affect their thoughts, feelings, and actions in that way.

Turning on her Positive Emotional Memory Disc and developing a HOOK are some of the strategies that earned Samantha M. a promotion to a high level of management. Prior to training with us, Samantha struggled with nerves any time she had to make an executive level presentation, and she was annoyed because she was unable to present herself in the best light possible. She found that taking time to insert her "Positive Emotional Memory Disk" before each presentation enabled her to exude the ease, authenticity, and confidence that came with these memories. Samantha also found that learning to Hook gave her a moment to breathe and convince her audience that she was prepared and confident.

Samantha told us that her first meeting post training was entirely different. She stood with authority, was centered, made calm, direct eye contact, and used an intelligent, well-thought-out hook to engage her audience. It was as if confidence flooded back and she proceeded to deliver the information in absolute comfort and in her zone. This directly resulted in an opportunity for a promotion to a higher level of management when she was seen as more confident, competent, and capable. In fact, whenever Samantha sees us, she makes of point of saying that she owes the continuing success of her career to these *small Changes.*

ALWAYS TUNE IN TO **WIIFM–** *What's In It For Me?*

The fact of the matter is that everyone is tuned into WIIFM, "What's in it for me?" The "ME" in this situation is your audience. It's not selfishness; it's human nature. Consequently, if you constantly remind your audience of the benefit or value you are providing to them, or their company, or to an issue they are concerned with, you are more likely to attract and hold their attention.

Plan to give your audience the "benefit" early. Essentially, you need to answer the most important audience question at the beginning of every presentation. They're wondering, *"What's in this for me?"* and *"Why should I watch/ listen?"*

Let them know the benefit of paying close attention to you right up front – but do it in a way that grabs their attention.

Example: You don't want to say something bland and too obvious like: "The reason for this presentation is to persuade you to buy this software package because it will increase your sales." Rather, pose an interesting question involving a number, such as "Did you know that switching to automated sales software can increase your revenue by as much as seventy-five percent?" Note that using numbers, especially dollar amounts or percentages, adds power to your statements.

When you want people to agree with you, it is vital to accentuate the positives before conceding the negatives. In this way, you've elevated their decision-making framework up to the heights, and they can measure the negatives against those positives. Since everyone is tuned into WIIFM, if you aren't broadcasting on their station, they won't hear a word you say.

EVIDENCE & ANECDOTES: *Get the Facts and Tell the Story*

Find the most compelling evidence to support your message. It can come in the form of data, facts, statistics, or anecdotes (personal stories).

Example: If we want to persuade our audience to be more conscious of multi-platform marketing, we need to give them examples of top companies doing it more effectively, or give them statistics of the increased numbers of customers connected to these platforms of marketing. You can also disprove common misconceptions, provide thought provoking numbers, or post a number and ask the audience to guess what it represents relative to your topic. Remember, this needs to reinforce what you want them thinking, feeling, and doing.

The secret behind any memorable presentation, and the one technique that really gives you an edge, is the ability to tell great stories that make a point related to the topic.

Shape your stories so that they have a **P-A-L:**

- Point
- Anecdote
- Learning

– for the audience. Often the most memorable and impactful stories have an edge that may be in the form of humor, emotion, or providing perspective on the topic

Example: We often relate how a newly arrived friend of Nadia's ruined her new car by pumping it full of diesel instead of regular gas. Asked why he went so far as to physically force the unfamiliar nozzle into the gas tank, the friend responded, "I really didn't think about it." What was left unsaid was that he did not think it was necessary to *ask for help*. As a result, it cost thousands of dollars to repair the engine; but the incident also serves as a priceless cautionary tale that lends itself very neatly to a P-A-L:

- **Point** – The point of the presentation is to emphasize the importance of being willing to ask for assistance or information.

- **Anecdote** – This anecdote neatly illustrates the consequences of a "do-it-yourself" approach to a new situation.

- **Learning** – Reminds the audience in a some-what humorous way of the dire consequences of "going it alone".

It is interesting that people have no problem mentioning evidence and anecdotes in coffee talk or casual conversations, but they forget to purposefully include them as powerful tools of persuasion when kicking off a presentation.

REEL IN

The very best finish is the one that gives the audience something specific to do next. Make your call to action something like "Send me an e-mail." "Plan your next steps," or "Be prepared to go through them here next week."

Like hooking a fish, this is your final chance to "land" your audience and deliver on what it is you want from them, before you lose the floor and they can slip away. Like any persuasive presentation, your Reel In, or conclusion, is your opportunity to briefly summarize your presenta-tion, recommend action steps, and, finally, remind your audience why they will benefit by following your recommendations. For conven-ience, you can break your Reel-In down into the following three parts:

EXERCISE: *Develop a Reel-In by doing the following*:

- What we've looked at today is...

- What I'm asking you to do is...

- The benefit to you will be...

Another way of looking at your entire presentation, and the concluding Reel In, is to remember to ask yourself the question, *"What do I want my audience Thinking, Feeling, and Doing **(TFD)** as a result of our time here?"*

Lastly, never do a Q&A at the very end of your presentation; it zaps the energy. If you do want to have a Q & A, schedule it for the second-to-last item of your presentation. And time it carefully so that you can still end with that all-important Reel In that ultimately is intended to achieve the purpose of your speech or presentation.

In a presentation to industry peers on the importance of human resources in leading an organization, Kat's focus on hooking her audience with a provocative question and on what she wanted them "Thinking, Feeling and Doing" made all the difference in helping her connect.

She went into the presentation planning to detail specific ways that human resources leaders could improve the talent in their organization, but after talking to the members of the audience, she found what was really on their minds was the economy and the constant changes in their companies, which included mergers and acquisitions, bankruptcies, and changes in ownership.

Kat recognized that the audience desired a slightly different version of her message. Instead of providing the technical content she'd prepared, she realized that what she really wanted the audience Thinking, Feeling, and

Doing was to be more comfortable and confident in their ability to survive these changes, and the importance of their roles leading their organizations. Had she stayed with her original plan, it would have been a good presentation, but with the revised focus, it was more relevant and effective. Not only had she tuned in to what the audience needed and incorporated that into her message, but she was also very clear on what she wanted them thinking, feeling, and doing as a result.

Kat also made an immediate connection with her audience by asking the following question: "By a show of hands, how many of you in this room are going through a merger, an acquisition, a bankruptcy or a change in ownership?" There were very few people without their hands raised. She built on that connection and the presentation was a BIG success.

While the presentation started strong with the Hook of asking how many people had gone through one of these changes, it ended even more powerfully through the following Reel-In: "What we have focused on today is that you are not alone in the changes you are going through. What I am asking you to do is go back to your employees, your peers, and your organization's leadership, and share this perspective with them. This will position you as a leader who has the confidence and the capability to take on greater responsibility, and continue to move up as your organization evolves."

DELIVERY – THE POWER OF HOW

With your content set, the next step is to carry out your presentation with stellar delivery skills. How you deliver your speech is just as important as the content. You can actually plan how you want your audience to perceive you. This is where your awareness of all of the elements of nonverbal communication has the most impact. These elements include how you dress, walk into the room, gesture, and hold yourself.

Professor Albert Meharabian from UCLA has extensively studied the effects of nonverbal communication. He found that over 90% of the way a message is received is due to nonverbal cues. Whether you are intending to walk into the room and up to the podium when you are introduced, or whether you will be standing up front waiting for people to sit down and start paying attention, use body language that conveys passion, authority, and approachability. Also, project energy and enthusiasm.

As the venerable British Educator, Thomas Arnold said, "The difference between one man and another is not mere ability – it is energy."

It is not an accident that many broadcast journalists, politicians, and accomplished executives project energy and dynamism. For some, it is natural, but for many, it is a practiced effort to project high energy and command a room or audience.

- How do you project energy, authority, and enthusiasm, even on difficult days?

The answer is to use your body and your space to your advantage.

EXERCISE:

1. Take a deep breath and move your ribcage up: It will work wonders for your posture.

2. Be aware of your facial expression: a fixed smile can start to look like a grimace.

3. If you are sitting, minimize the barriers. And don't wiggle. Hold yourself with grace and confidence.

4. Take up space in the room: Stand with your legs apart and physically use different areas of the room. If you stand with your feet together, you look like a tapered candle that can be tipped over.

5. Be aware of your stance: Stand with your hips parallel to your feet. This is called "being rooted," and it gives the impression of a grounded, confident individual.

6. Combine this stance with a lower tone of voice, strong projection, and clothes that have structure, and you will have created an impression of stature and credibility.

We are often asked about how to move around the front of the room, or if you even should, during a presentation. Movement is good as long as you move with purpose and make the right moves. For example, don't back away or walk backward directly opposite your audience. This move zaps energy; rather, walk with the purpose of connecting with the audience.

Don't rock side-to-side or take constant steps – you'll look nervous and you'll make everyone else dizzy. This is often an unconscious habit people have, so video yourself, and if this is you, be aware of it and work on planting your feet firmly on the ground.

One very effective move is to take two or three steps before pausing to ground your position. Then take a few steps again, pause and ground your position, and point.

To keep the rhythm going, think to yourself: "*Step, Step, and Pause. Step, Step, Pause.*"

Taking timed steps is also a way to control the pacing of your presentation. While you don't want to talk and present information so quickly that your audience has trouble following, you also don't want to be too slow, especially when it comes to PowerPoint presentations. Keeping any one slide up too long is a surefire way to lose the attention of your audience. Videotaping and timing your presentation ahead of time is a good strategy to ensure that your pacing, like the porridge for Goldilocks, is "just right" for the audience.

As it relates to movement, body language, or gestures, remember this: Anything, even the funniest phrase or the most powerful hand gestures, when done in excess, can become distracting. Mix it up and find a way to get comfortable with your surroundings.

As long as you are confident that you have included all of the relevant information and action steps that your presentation requires, don't be concerned if your speech seems too short. Nobody complains about short present-ations; it's the overlong and windy versions that elicit groans, boredom, and a tuned out audience. Start on time and end early. Leave them wanting more, not dying of boredom.

In terms of projecting an aura of calm and authority, make sure that either your nerves, or movements, do not result in visibly sweaty armpits. If you are an excessive sweater, you may benefit from medical advice and a prescription-strength deodorant. If you are concerned about this, be sure to adjust your wardrobe so that your clothing does not show damp spots in a stressful situation. In these cases, remember that that black fabric is certainly your friend.

What should you do with your hands? It is often helpful to hold something in one hand, like a PowerPoint remote, or your note cards. And, on the topic of PowerPoints, it is very helpful to have your own remote slide changer: Each one is different, and using one you are comfortable with is a great stress reducer. Also use your hands to help your brain, and gesture to show your passion.

Hand gestures help you to stress certain words, give them vitality, and help to add variations of modulation and pitch. How you use your hands can also convey volumes in terms of nonverbal communication. Open hand movements convey a sense of power, while open hands with the palms facing up signal that you are inviting, but humble. If you steeple your hands, you are conveying a combination of power and humility. And if you strike the "beggar's pose", with your palms facing in front of you, this communicates a sense of openness. If you keep your hands below your hips, people don't notice them, and you won't get credit for your great use of hand gestures.

It is also important to be aware of gestures and hand movements that are likely to be perceived negatively. For example, if you wave your hands above your shoulders, it is very likely that you could be perceived as a little out of control. And while some audiences respond to a healthy dose of wild energy, we don't recommend it for most formal presentations. Hands above the head are used for workouts and ground traffic control for inbound aircraft, not professional presentations. Similarly, tight fists, hand smacks, and assertive chopping movements are also perceived as threatening and aggressive.

While these descriptions are certainly generalizations of possible interpretations, it adds another tool in your presentation toolbox to understand how your audience may react to something. They may also help explain any feedback or change in engagement you may sense in your audience.

Make a point of practicing your moves before you take them in front of an audience. If possible, have a friend video you to make sure that the use of your body enhances, rather than detracts, from your presentation. It is also very helpful to watch a well-known public speaker in action and take notes: How do they use their space, hands, and voice?

Using your voice effectively also contributes to powerful presentations. Be sure you are using a volume that can be clearly heard from all areas of the room. In large rooms, using a lavaliere microphone is helpful, as it can be positioned for the best quality sound without you having to adjust it.

If you have a handheld microphone, be aware that it likely needs to be held closer to your mouth than you think, but holding it too close can result in a muffled and irritating vocal projection.

If you have no microphone, prior to your presentation, ask someone to sit in various areas of the room and run through a few sentences to be sure they can hear you. Be aware of any noisy equipment such as coolers, air conditioners, fans, or activities in a nearby room or hall that may require you to step up the volume. A trick to handle unexpected noises is to go to a table discussion or activity for the group while the noise passes. If this isn't possible do your best to read the audience's ability to pay attention, acknowledge the distraction, and more forward with grace.

Reminder: When it comes to scripting your presentation, never start with the words, "What I am going to talk about today is..." or you'll set up the expectation in your audience that this presentation is going to be a bore fest. Rather, hook your audience within the first few seconds with a question, compelling statement, or interesting fact.

The depth and quality of your speaking voice are important indicators of how confident you are. The good news is you can improve both depth and quality, and calm yourself down at the same time, by becoming more aware of your breathing. If you are nervous, it is likely that your breathing will be quick and shallow, and your voice will be high and squeaky. More slow deep breaths will help you speak more audibly, and also lower the register of your voice.

Have you ever noticed what a pitcher does on the baseball mound? He blows out slowly – this is another simple breathing strategy that will help you to calm down and focus.

Be sure to warm up your voice before a major meeting, presentation, or interview. If you breathe, hum, articulate, and practice, your voice will come across more authoritatively. We do this all the time, and it makes a noticeable difference. While it's not an option if you use public transportation, use your time in the car on your way to a morning meeting or presentation to warm up your voice:

EXERCISE:
   Warm up your voice:
   Hamm amm amm
   Hemm emm emm
   Himm imm imm
   Homm omm omm
   Humm umm umm
   Sally Sells Sea Shells By The Sea Shore

Diminish the use of "fillers" – those "ums", "ahs", and "you knows". They are the hallmarks of an inexperienced or nervous public speaker. Just like snoring, you may not be aware of the extent to which you use "fillers", and it would be helpful to have a colleague or friend observe you, and note how many times you revert to these rather annoying verbal tics while making a presentation. You'll probably be shocked by the number, but this will surely help you to make a conscious effort to avoid them. A pause, on the other hand, especially after an important point, can be powerful. Use strategic pauses when appropriate. They are good for emphasis, and they also give your audience a chance to absorb the information you are communicating.

A well-placed pause also goes well with opportunities for eye contact. Making consistent, three-second meaningful eye contact with the members of your audience helps reinforce your authority, sincerity, and creates a true connection with them. If your audience numbers in the hundreds or thousands, focus on a few individuals in various areas of the room. Although you are gazing in a general area, it gives a much more personal feel, as if you are looking at many people, and not just one that you are focusing on. Some professionals have been told to stare at the back of the room in large presentations, but that conveys a sense that you are looking past the audience and not connecting with them. Eye contact is all about making connection and creating engagement.

And in the event that you forget your words or make a mistake, pretend that this is actually a well-rehearsed pause, or come back with a quip like, "Let me reconnect my mind to my mouth" or, even better, ask the group a question to give yourself a moment to reconnect your brain. We have both made funny and sometimes embarrassing slips. One of the funniest was substituting the word "sex" for "text". If that happens to you, smile, say "moving on", and continue with your presentation.

Projecting authority is particularly challenging for youthful speakers, and Lisa R., one of our younger clients, complained that she wasn't given the opportunity to do sales presentations because her manager felt she lacked authority and credibility. This was reflected in how she spoke in meetings.

We worked with her to eliminate the words "like", "you-know," and "um" in her verbal communication, to stand in a more grounded position without crossing her legs, and to make more open arm gestures. We also helped her to lower her voice by doing a series of resonance and breathing exercises. Those *small Changes* had an astounding effect, and Lisa is now thriving in ad sales.

So, rather than avoiding presentations, treat them as a golden opportunity to stand out from the pack and enhance your professional presence.

Recap: We have put together this handy checklist with pointers that can help you stand out and give powerful presentations.

- **Do a voice warm-up before a major meeting, presentation, or interview:** breathe, hum, articulate, and practice. You will be calmer, and your voice will come across as more authoritative.

- **Use powerful open hand movements**.

- **Be aware of your stance:** Standing with your hips parallel to your feet gives the impression of a grounded, confident individual.

- **Move with purpose:** Take two to three steps, then pause and ground your position; then take a few steps again, and pause and ground your position and point.

- **Diminish the use of "fillers" like "um", "ah", and "you know".** Have someone watch you and make a note of every time you say your "filler" word. Make a conscious effort to reduce those moments.

- **Make consistent three-second meaningful eye contact.**

- **Air your armpits**, and if all else fails, be sure to wear clothing that doesn't reveal perspiration stains.

- **Take up space in the room:** Stand with your legs apart and physically use different areas of the room.

- **Don't back away or walk backward directly opposite your audience**; it zaps energy. Rather, walk side to side.

- **If you forget your words, or make a mistake, come back with a quip,** or ask the group a question to give yourself a moment to reconnect your brain.

- **Don't be afraid of pauses.** They are powerful and give your audience a chance to take in the information.

- **Don't rock side to side or take constant steps**; you'll look nervous and you'll make everyone else dizzy.

Watch a tape of yourself to find out if you do this, or any of the previous distracting movements, then correct them accordingly.

The *small Changes*:

- Engage your audience immediately by using a "hook."

- Define your message and content in the most succinct way.

- Get emotional buy in and participation through well-told anecdotes (personal stories).

- End with a Reel In, call to action, or benefit statement.

The *BIG IMPACT*: You will always make a strong impression when speaking in front of groups and the perception of you as a leader will be greatly enhanced.

CHAPTER 3

IT'S ALL IN THE PACKAGING: How to Impress, Dress, and Stress Less to Give Yourself Maximum Impact

Every little thing we do and say communicates who we are. There are volumes of psychological studies that demonstrate the extent to which we fill in the blanks, using our experience, prior knowledge, and yes, prejudices to make subconscious judgments about the people we encounter, and do business with. It is a natural response, based on the very adaptive human need to make quick decisions about the people we meet: *"Should I trust and rely on them? Are they important? Or are they dangerous?"*

Our advice is to never judge someone by his or her appearance. You never know who you may be talking to, or how they can be impactful in your life. However, although we wish everyone would follow that advice, they don't. And, while you can't immediately change the filter through which others view the world, you can understand best practices in making positive impressions with your physical presence no matter what the audience or situation.

The process of forming a first impression occurs in every new situation. Within the first few seconds, people pass judgment on you, and it can sometimes be a difficult opinion to reverse. First impressions are one of those small things that make a *BIG IMPACT*, so there is not much margin for error.

Remember, in the absence of alternative information, people generally come to their own conclusions, so you have to send messages about who you are in every way possible to provide that needed information and impression.

Example: Try to read the following passage:

A sutdy wsa dnoe by Cmiarbdge Uinrevtisy taht shoewd that as lnog as the frsit and lsat lteetrs wree the smae, msot ivnidialus cluod raed waht was in fnrot of tehm.

Tihs is bceusae yuor mnid deos not raed eervy ltteer, but rtaher mkaes qiuck jdugnmet bsead on waht you see as a wolhe.

This study was not actually conducted at Cambridge University, and if you do not speak

English as a first language, and the consonants were more scrambled, this would not work as smoothly. Nevertheless, it does illustrate the extent to which we bring subconscious assumptions to the way we perceive incomplete information. In effect, our minds literally fill in the blanks.

Why can you read it so easily? The passage does not start "A study was done", but that's what you assume it should be, based on a split-second assumption that the words are simply misspelled. Indeed, if we scrambled common words in any language but kept the first and last letters and most of the consonants the same, we could likely read a similarly scrambled passage with ease.

Now, try reading the following:

Iamigne waht yuor mnid deos when yuo see a prseon and waht thye're weranig, fnid out a presnol triat, or wacth bdoy lagnauge. Yuro mnid prjeugdes; it's jsut nartual.

These are the kinds of judgments you make when you meet a person for the first time, and take note of what that individual is wearing, or what kind of body language he or she is displaying. Your mind prejudges, and whether you are aware of it or not, places the person into a particular social, economic, and professional pigeonhole. Researchers have found that a person's appearance and body language – the nature of their Physical Presence – actually has more impact on how we assess and judge that person than what we know about that individual's qualifications or what they have to say.

In fact, Robert B. Cialdini, who has conducted extensive studies on the science of influencing and persuasion, says we trust people who make us feel protected. That is why it is so important to project a sense of solidity, authority, and stature, even if you are only five feet tall.

Moreover, Dr. Albert Mehrabian, a social psychologist famed for his studies of the effects of nonverbal communication, is frequently quoted for his findings: 7% of the way a message is received is composed of actual words we use; 38% is communicated through the tone of our voice and voice inflection, and 55% comes from our nonverbal communication. At the end of the day, you can't really quantify the human brain like that, but there's no question that most of the way we receive a message is through nonverbal cues.

This study, and many other like it, simply confirm that everything we do communicates, and a lack of congruency between WHAT you are saying VERBALLY, and your PHYSICAL PRESENCE undermines your ability to be powerful and credible.

Like it or not, your physical appearance is an important part of the impact of the overall impression you make on people. For example, if one of your new colleagues was to walk into a meeting wearing a button-down cardigan sweater with a turtleneck underneath, loose fitting pants and flat loafers, what assumptions would you make about that person? Conservative, meek, quiet? You didn't even see a picture, but is it likely that you thought of some variation of that characterization.

What if an employee arrived at an early morning training session with wet hair, creased, un-hemmed pants and a grubby white shirt? She's a hard worker, but would you put her first in line for a promotion or an unexpected opportunity to meet with a new client, boss, or partner? What if the leaders walked in to talk with the team that day? Probably not. These are the little opportunities that get missed over time. This is about making the most of unexpected and potentially meaningful opportunities.

Now, imagine the effect if the same individual had walked into the session with her hair tied back, and wearing a black tailored blazer and heels. It wouldn't matter if she was also wearing jeans, pants or a skirt. The effect of the blazer and heels instantly gives her an aura of being pulled together, and having authority. Why is that? An individual can wear a fluffy sweater and still be highly capable, but the message is likely to get lost in a sea of other assumptions.

Think about it. Why do policemen, pilots, and security guards wear uniforms? Why does the President of the United States always wear a dark suit to press conferences and important meetings?

The answer is that these types of clothing give them **S-P-F:**

Structure
Proportion
Fit

If you were to ask most people to visualize successful, powerful, and trustworthy individuals, often those images would be of people who appear well pulled together. The structured nature of the person's wardrobe and image conveys messages of authority, reliability, and organization. In essence, garments that give you Structure are more likely to create the image of Proportion and Fit than those without structure. How do you use these principles in today's wide variety of business environments to create the most impactful professional presence?

Simply: Pay attention to Structure, Proportion and Fit. Even if you work in an environment where "business casual" is the norm, it's still advantageous to wear garments that provide some form of S-P-F.

To be considered for a promotion opportunity that involves taking on more responsibilities or making strong first impressions, your superiors have to be able to physically envision you at a different level. Of course, this is not always the case. There are some very successful "slobs" out there, but they usually are in a position where their skill set is in high demand, and their job description does not usually involve interacting with the public.

Moreover, this book is about taking advantage of every possible opportunity you can, which means using all the tools and techniques available to you to create an impactful impression. The intention is to make people want to listen to you, get to know you, and believe they can trust you, so that you can develop a greater competitive edge in work and life. For this reason, even if the usual dress code in your office is jeans and sneakers, always opt for the well-fitting versions and to be on the more professional end of what is acceptable. You might as well take advantage of the stature that more formal, well-structured clothing gives you.

Even if your company observes Casual Fridays, don't dress for work as if you're heading out to a tiki bar. Rather, think about wearing khakis and the best fitting jeans, and definitely avoid wearing T-shirts that advertise the latest video game, or inform everybody where you went on your last vacation.

However, if wearing a T-shirt is the norm, at least wear a solid color that fits well. It's a way to add to the overall perception of your personal brand with minimal effort. You never know what kinds of opportunities could be coming your way, and for that matter, it is important to be aware of the extent to which your appearance could be sabotaging your job success.

Your Appearance Could Be Sabotaging Your Success

Example: Melanie P. worked as a trainer for a large company, and was in danger of losing her job. While management felt that her training skills were very good, her dress, which consisted of loose, baggy-looking garments and long, shaggy hair, did not communicate the professionalism the company wanted. In addition, she tended to slouch and looked bored in meetings, which also contributed to a negative impression.

Melanie felt that her technical expertise spoke for itself and that structured clothing was reserved for church and social events. She had always seen work as a place where she had to show expertise, and wrongly underestimated the importance of physical appearance at her job. We worked with Melanie to help her internalize the importance of nonverbal communication, using video and visual examples to show her how quickly she herself made snap judgments of people based on first impressions.

The *small Changes* she made were to have her hair cut in a current style and to wear garments that were tailored to the shape of her body. She also improved her posture and exhibited attentive facial expressions during meetings.

The *BIG IMPACT?* Not a day goes by, she told us, when people don't comment on her transformed appearance, and most importantly, she has not only kept her job but received two substantial promotions within the space of just a few months.

You never know what might be coming your way.

Example: In the early stages of her career, Kat was asked, on short notice, to sit on a panel of experts at the headquarters of a local, well-known company. Kat wasn't told much about who was on the panel; nevertheless, she happily agreed, even though her schedule was tight for that day and she had worked late the night before. Although she was tempted to wear the business casual clothes she had on, she decided to swing by her home and change into a suit instead. Little did Kat know that this panel consisted of the presidents of several major companies, and that the host was a top-level headhunter.

It was a golden opportunity to impress, and Kat was in a position to take advantage of it by showing up in style. In fact, the business and career connections that she made at that panel led to meaningful relationships that have served her and her companies well over the years. A few of the audience members recommended her for job opportunities immediately following the event. She turned them down, but she'd clearly made a *BIG impression*.

Dress professionally, but appropriately. You also don't want to be drawing too much attention to yourself. Always pay attention to the "dress culture" and who your customers are so that you avoid wearing anything that interferes with their ability to trust you.

Example: If you are a social worker in a major teaching hospital, it's not a good idea to discuss discharge planning with the family of a patient while wearing a tight mini skirt and bright red nails. That draws attention to things that you don't want people noticing most about you in the workplace. Remember it's best to be less obsessed with looking "incredible", and more with looking "credible".

We aren't suggesting that the same dress code applies to every situation; rather, we want to emphasize the importance of paying attention to your environment and knowing yourself. We're giving you simple strategies to make the most out of your physical presence in a range of scenarios so that you can present an image of confidence and credibility.

Take a look at this personal checklist:

- **How many of these steps have you taken already** to ensure that you can always make an impression that has impact and maximizes use of Structure-Proportion-Fit? And how many do you need to add to your repertoire?

- **Take note of what shape and size you are**, and be conscious of the effect you have. For example, if you are very tall, be aware that you can be intimidating.

- **Balance your presence:** if you are large in size, bright colors and big buttons may not be for you in most situations; you do not want to overpower people.

- **If you are small in size**, accessories and details in your clothing can you give more of a presence.

- **Ladies, avoid wearing skirts that are too short**, or tops that are too low.

- **Acquire a go-to blazer or jacket** that you can wear over jeans, pants, or a skirt: black, grey, or navy are staples.

- **Whatever the dress code, clothing that has shape and structure** will almost always do the trick. Make sure that your wardrobe includes shirts with collars and at least one structured jacket.

- **Choose clothes with clean lines and in classic colors,** like navy, grey, and black – and always check the length of your pants.

- **If you are a lady with a large bust, don't challenge the laws of physics** with the buttons on your shirts. They will lose that battle every time. Figure out what fits you, and find tops that won't physically deconstruct when you move or take a deep breath.

- **Similarly, if you are a large male, be sure to size your clothing** so that it doesn't look strained.

Not everyone is a supermodel. Know your body and how clothes fit you. If you have some areas of your body that are tough to dress, do the best you can. Go to a department store and ask for advice from a knowledgeable salesperson.

Find a store or brand of clothing that consistently works for you.

You don't need to spend a lot of money, but you may find that an investment in one or two well-tailored pieces of clothing will be the best purchase you have made in a while. They can be real time-savers if you need to put something together quickly for an important event.

Have you ever looked at others and wondered if they stopped to look at themselves? Get dressed in front of a full-length mirror.

Don't let your issues with body image or appearance give you the excuse to let other things go. Iron your clothes, polish your shoes, and pull yourself together with style.

Eye contact, hygiene, and polished shoes are similar in one important way: they are not luxuries; they are necessities.

- Find a good, cost-effective tailor: you can buy $20 pants and make them look like they cost $200 if they fit you well. (Kat loves going to thrift stores and discount retailers and finding pants that don't quite fit and seeing the transformation that her tailor in Atlanta can make with a needle and some thread.)

- Follow the rule of gum, food stains, and wrinkled clothes: Get rid of them; they zap your authority.

- Be sure your undergarments are never visible. Know how your clothes move when you move, and make sure that they don't reveal any secrets.

- Keep a small sewing kit and double-sided fabric tape handy for emergency clothing repairs.

Although there is much more to projecting a compelling Physical Presence than dress alone, this is clearly an area in which you can easily make a difference, and it is a key element of the package over which you have control. When you have the confidence that you project a professional appearance, you are also likely to develop the posture, grace, and confidence that can give you a vital advantage in any situation.

The *small Changes* you can make to show up and move up are:

- Structure your appearance so that you are ready for the opportunities that can come every day and at any time.

- Dress for your particular body.

- Decide how you can be appropriate and credible.

- Get dressed in front of a mirror: if you have questions or doubts, the answer is "no".

The *BIG IMPACT*: You will be perceived as highly credible, polished, and poised.

CHAPTER 4

FOCUS ON THE INTERPERSONAL: Using Poise and Professionalism to Handle the small Things before they become BIG Issues

The way you are perceived is the culmination of many factors. Key among these is your ability to relate to others in the most effective, powerful, and gracious way. And even more revealing is how you navigate the inevitable interpersonal conflicts that arise in the workplace.

Not surprisingly, handling and defusing interpersonal conflicts in the workplace can be immensely challenging for various reasons.

First, you may be able to choose your friends, but you are generally not in charge of selecting who will be your colleagues or boss. When a coworker behaves in a way that upsets or hurts you, you can't necessarily walk away in the hopes that you will never have to deal with him or her again.

Second, even though emotions can run high, particularly if you feel you are being unfairly singled out or criticized, the open expression of negative emotions – otherwise known as yelling and screaming, rolling eyes, or pounding fists – is frankly not acceptable in most work environments, and can make a bad situation much, much worse.

Take a moment and think about the last time you experienced a situation where you disagreed with someone, or someone did something that you perceived as irritating, upsetting or insensitive.

- How did you handle it?

- And what was the outcome?

- Did you resolve the conflict amicably and find resolution?

- Or did it end in further conflict and alienation?

The fact is we have a choice to either be a part of the issue, or the problem solver. The challenge is to strive to become the latter in such a way that you can accomplish at least three things:

- Defuse the conflict,

- Find a constructive solution, and

- Maintain your self-respect.

This helps build your reputation as a problem solver and someone who others want to work with. As Robert Frost wisely said: "You are educated when you have the ability to listen to almost anything without losing your temper and/ or self-confidence." If you can keep your cool, particularly, as Rudyard Kipling wrote, "when all about you are losing theirs and blaming it on you", then you will come out better every time.

The first step is to literally take a step – backwards.

Don't immediately react:

- Rather, employ that tried and true calming measure of taking a deep breath and, if necessary, "counting to ten".

- Then, if you can wait a day before responding, even better.

This does not mean you should completely avoid the problem and hope it will go away. Conflicts that are not addressed are likely to fester and cause long-term problems. Rather, use the time to do as Stephen Covey says in *The Seven Habits of Highly Effective People*: "Seek first to understand before being understood." Then try to analyze the source of the problem. The origins of the conflict might not even be as personal as you may think.

According to Alice Fuscaldo, the employee relations and training specialist for IEEE Human Resources, in Piscataway, N.J., "Sometimes conflicts arise from a scarcity of time, money, workers, supplies, or other resources. Or there might be a communication problem, especially when your colleagues don't understand exactly what is required of them, or vice versa."

Be honest with yourself: If you are one of those people who consistently experiences conflict and tension from job to job, our advice is to evaluate the common denominator, which may involve taking a tough look in the mirror. Simply stated, be open to the possibility that the source of the conflicts may be you.

In fact, that was exactly the case with a television producer who Nadia knew well. Melissa S. was very good at her job and had excellent technical skills, but was constantly frustrating others and in situations of conflict. For her, the workplace was a battlefield and every experience an act of war. Melissa's response to even the slightest criticism and disagreement was almost always becoming defensive. Sadly, in all her years, she never learned how to deflect, how to defuse conflict, and how to come to a solution. As a result, tremendous time was wasted, and many feelings were hurt. Melissa became the person no one wanted to work with and eventually she was fired.

An extremely useful strategy is to always live by the tenet of ASSUMING POSITIVE INTENT. In essence, instead of immediately getting angry, or making an assumption about where the other person is coming from, take a moment to consider the situation from his or her perspective. Then proceed from the assumption that this individual really intends to "do the right thing". This may seem to be counterintuitive. As human beings, we instinctively defend ourselves, and if we perceive we are being attacked, we assume the worst, and our defense can come across as aggressive.

Often, the person who is causing your distress will be disarmed by your conciliatory attitude. Most people expect an aggressive response because they are ready for a fight. But if you respond with an "I am so sorry, there seems to be some misunderstanding here... help me understand how we can resolve this?" Or try this powerful question: "Can you tell me a little more about what's behind this?" You will be amazed at their reaction. Keep in mind that this is not "wimping out". Rather, you will be responding from a position of strength, not weakness, for you are the one who has made a conscious choice to seek constructive solutions, rather than to win a war. The alternative is staying in a mode of conflict, and being viewed as less productive, polished, and accomplished than you really are. You always have a choice. The war you are winning is one of your reputation and credibility; being seen as an effective collaborator and problem solver is immensely powerful in the overall trajectory of your life and career.

In the early stages of her career as head of International Training and Development for a multi-national hospitality company, Kat herself experienced the negative impact of being over-emotional. She was leading a training and research initiative in her company to add a new menu segment when she was told that the executives had decided to rush the project and not provide the necessary training. Kat was very upset, and called the executive in question, making it obvious that she was very concerned. His response was, "Sometimes you need to throw things against the wall and see if they stick." She responded strongly to what she perceived as his dismissive attitude, and the call did not end positively.

Almost immediately Kat realized that she had come across as overly emotional, and did not make the most of that opportunity to talk directly with the executive. After that conversation, Kat noticed that she was being excluded from many of the executive level discussions.

At that point, Kat realized that she could either pout and feel it was unfair that her perspective was not being valued – or she could recognize that the tone of her voice and the energy she conveyed created a divide between herself and this executive. She then spent several weeks asking questions and seeking understanding, while still holding true to her business opinions to add value to the group.

By presenting herself in this way, she conveyed more balance and poise to reposition herself as a partner whom they would want to have involved in the project. Over time, this executive and Kat developed stronger rapport. She was then included in all the necessary meetings going forward, and she learned a valuable lesson: It's not what you say; it's how you say it. Allowing emotion to override thoughtful content in a conversation can have damaging effects on not only relationships, but potentially your career and future opportunities.

Personality issues such as ego, selfishness, or personal differences also play an important role in work conflicts. Consequently, in the important quest of "keeping your cool" you will find it very helpful if you can develop the ability to see the world from the other person's point of view. It's common to make the assumption that everyone sees things the way you do, rather than taking into account that people from different backgrounds and with different personality styles handle situations differently. This is where developing Emotional Intelligence, otherwise known as your EQ, becomes important for both your survival and success in any environment.

Most people have a tendency to connect immediately with people who have a disposition similar to their own. But your work colleagues are not usually your closest friends. Therefore, if you are an outgoing extrovert, you may find it a challenge to negotiate with quieter, more reserved people. Equally, if you are very social and people orientated, a coworker who is totally focused on work and getting the job done may at first appear cold and uninterested in the emotional dimensions of an issue.

It is in these moments of judgment where you need to remind yourself that differences in personality style, although not always obvious at first, can be as vast and divisive as differences in age, background, and culture.

Take a careful look at yourself by asking:

- "What kind of personality do I bring to the table?"

- "Do I respond defensively to criticism and have a need to always be right?"

- "Am I always in a hurry to get the job done?"

- "Do I find it hard to wait while other people catch up with my understanding of the issue and the approach I would like to take?"

- "Is it always the fault of someone else?"

That was the attitude that almost got Alex Y., an Atlanta area media editor, into trouble. Alex found himself being hauled over the coals for his rough, abrasive manner with producers. True, the producers often asked him to do things without also giving him the necessary instructions and tools. Instead of explaining what he needed to be productive, Alex would simply get aggressive and angry. Eventually, Alex was told that if he had another conflict with somebody, he would be written up.

Alex came to our class, and we were able to show him that there is always a way of dealing with an issue that is more solution-oriented. He learned to be more explicit about what he needed, and to communicate these needs in a rational manner that did not pin the blame on other people. As a result, Alex created far better relationships, and has become an important asset to the department.

Dr. Tony Alessandra, a seasoned marketing guru, points out that it is only by understanding the nuances through which other individuals see the world that we can begin to relate to them in a meaningful way. When you treat people the way YOU want to be treated, you create relationship tension. When you treat people the way THEY want to be treated, you build RAPPORT.

Your ability to build rapport and relate to as many personality styles as possible is one of the most valuable qualities you can possess. To do this, it is important to learn how to read your work colleagues' verbal, vocal (voice inflection) and visual signals, and then adapt your behavior to accommodate their behavioral style.

Dr. Alessandra has identified four basic personality styles:

- Directors
- Socializers
- Relaters
- Thinkers

The **Director**, for example, is results orientated, decisive, and direct, while the **Thinker** is careful, detailed, and reserved. The **Relater** is likely to be friendly and avoid conflict, while the **Socializer** is enthusiastic and creative.

Dr. Alessandra suggests using a range of strategies to communicate effectively with people of different personalities, particularly in the case of conflict situations.

- For the **Director**, it is important to focus on results, give direct answers, and lower your expectations for an empathetic response to your particular issue.

- The **Thinker** prefers to be given as many details as possible, and appreciates time to gather information and decide on solutions. In a conflict situation, this person will need time to reflect on or digest the issue at hand before responding.

- The **Socializer** is not a detail person, and appreciates the freedom to plan and accomplish his or her work.

- The **Relater** values expressions of appreciation and support.

We obviously resonate and connect more with some people than others. Each and every one of us relates to people differently depending on our own personality style. Some of us are very open and share personal details quickly. Others are more reserved and would never think of discussing our personal lives on first meeting. There are those people who leave a meeting having noticed the tension that existed between two colleagues, and there are those so focused on the task at hand that this went by unnoticed.

To relate to people more successfully, and resolve conflicts and disagreements when they arise, it is important to learn how to read your coworkers' verbal, vocal (voice inflections), and visual signals, and then adapt your behavior to accommodate their behavioral style.

Some individuals find it easy to converse with strangers and will quickly share relatively personal information. Others are more reserved and may need time to feel comfortable in a new social situation before opening up. The more open person usually enjoys personal interaction that is warm and lively, and in the case of conflicts and disagreements, will probably be more receptive to honest discussions of the issue.

On the other hand, a more reserved individual is likely to shut down and "head for the hills" if approached too quickly when conflicts arise. This kind of individual will need time to think over the issue, and would probably respond well to a low-key, non-confrontational effort to solve the problem at hand. In addition, the "socializer" would probably respond positively to a "face-to-face" discussion of a contentious issue, while the more reserved individual, or "thinker" is likely to be more comfortable if you communicate with him or her by e-mail or text.

Individuals with different personality characteristics also prefer different kinds of communication styles. For example, people who have strong leadership qualities usually appreciate direct, results-oriented communication. A creative type, on the other hand, might respond well to communication that refers to his or her field of interest. This kind of individual may not be interested in details, but will appreciate being given time to plan and accomplish his or her own work.

Meanwhile, an introverted, detail-oriented individual is not likely to respond well to over-enthusiastic behavior that he or she feels is impinging on his or her personal space. This personality type will probably prefer to be given as many details as possible, and appreciates time to gather information and decide on solutions.

Some people value interpersonal relation-ships, while others are more comfortable as "loners." A person who is invested in inter-personal relationships may value expressions of appreciation and support, and be relatively comfortable dealing with interpersonal conflicts and disagreements. A "loner" may feel uncom-fortable in that kind of situation, and prefer a certain distance.

Recently, Kat's insight into how individuals with different personality styles can experience difficulty working together, plus her commitment to Assuming Positive Intent, helped defuse a potentially damaging conflict in her leadership team.

Gina and Rob frequently clashed, to the extent that Gina was threatening to leave if she had to continue working with him. The problem was that while Rob was very talented at the technical aspects of his job, he was also often tense, would yell a lot, and could be difficult to work with.

Kat's perception as a leader was that both of them had failed to use the necessary poise and professionalism to be effective in a fast-paced work environment. However, she also understood that in order to keep things moving quickly, they needed her support to work through their interpersonal challenges.

She had to acknowledge that Rob was an emotional guy: he had a short fuse, but he also took a great deal of pride in his work, and he had an unbelievably heavy workload. What became apparent to Kat was that both of them had a negative reaction to each other's personalities. Therefore, the tone, tenor, and negative energy of their conversations only escalated when they worked together.

Kat responded by having the members of her team take two personality assessments: both DISC (a personality assessment system that classifies individuals by four aspects of behavior – Dominance, Influence, Steadiness and Compliance) and the Myers-Briggs Personality Inventory. The members of the team then met to discuss the results, while agreeing to Assume Positive Intent.

The exercise helped Gina and Rob understand certain personally traits were not a personal affront or attack, but in fact a matter of personal style that just happened to cause conflict between them. While Gina was focused on details, Rob wanted to move quickly on to the next step, and became frustrated when that didn't happen. Once they understood that it wasn't personal, they both found a little more common ground that enabled them to work together more effectively.

In their meetings, Kat, who is herself a high energy person with a very dominant style, focused on being calm and clear to model the importance of tweaking your style when necessary. Although Gina and Rob continue to have some bumps in the road, they have since been able to work together more effectively and support each other in the workplace. In addition, both Gina and Rob were able to impress Kat with their ability to lead through conflict and conduct themselves professionally in an ever-changing workplace.

To summarize, when you develop the inter-personal skills to keep your cool and handle difficult interpersonal situations with grace and power, you will have met one of the most important challenges of attaining Professional Presence. Remember, the best way to disarm a conflict is to ASSUME POSITIVE INTENT and refuse to go to war.

The *small Changes* that can give you an advantage, both in the workplace and in your personal life as well are:

- Evaluate every situation Assuming Positive Intent.

- Do unto others as they would have done to themselves.

- Be gracious: conciliatory behavior will get you everywhere.

- Observe and respect different personality styles.

The *BIG IMPACT*: People will like you, trust you, and want to do business with you.

CHAPTER 5

SOCIAL PRESENCE: *How to Fine-Tune Your Networking Skills and Transform Connections into Rewarding Relationships*

You would not be reading this book if you didn't already appreciate the importance of relationship building in career success. The phrase "It's all about networking and connections," is one of those mantras that we all hear so often that it is probably embedded in your subconscious as well. In fact, we take it as a given that most of you have already engaged in some form of social networking in the educational, social, and work setting. The question is, "How do I improve and fine-tune my networking skills, and develop reciprocal and mutually advantageous professional relationships in the process?"

We begin by suggesting that you conceptualize your ability to network in social and business settings as a form of Social Presence. Building real, meaningful relationships, both within your existing network, as well as with new individuals, is critical to your career success. It is as much a part of maximizing your Personal Presence as your ability to make a great presentation or dress professionally.

TO FOLLOW IS A QUICK QUIZ TO ANALYZE YOUR OWN SOCIAL PRESENCE:

If you had a choice between attending a party or staying home and watching the latest episode of your favorite TV show, what would you choose?

_____

_____

You receive an invitation to a cocktail party honoring a long-time employee who is about to retire. What is your response?

_____

_____

You are attending a convention in which there will be presentations on the latest research in your field. The schedule includes a "mixer" before the presentation. How excited are you about it?

_____

_____

Do you play any team sports for fun? If so, which one(s)?

_____

_____

Do you belong to any volunteer organizations? If so, which one(s)?

_____

_____

Do you want to make more connections with people in your work and social environment, but you don't know how to start going about it?

_____

_____

Do your answers reveal:

- You prefer to avoid social events, and would rather stay home or in your hotel room, over developing work and social relationships?

- Would you really rather watch your favorite TV show?

- Do you break out in a sweat at the thought of starting a conversation with a stranger?

If so, you are not all that unusual! Many people get nervous at the prospect of "networking" and would rather not face up to the challenges of developing new relationships and connections. Their excuse might be, "I don't know how to connect with people who are out of my familiar social comfort zone." Or, "I find work-related social events boring." But what many people really mean is they dread making new friends and connections, because they are really unsure of how to behave.

So, how do you go about developing those "mutually reciprocal relationships based on the exchange of ideas, resources, and contacts"?

Here's how: You'll need to change your mindset.

Start to think of networking as a three-step process involving connections, conversations, and collaborations.

ADJUST YOUR ATTITUDE

Start off with an adjustment in your point of view.

First, you need to recognize that with very few exceptions, work is a social activity; it is often your social presence and interpersonal skills that will distinguish you from other equally qualified candidates. Thus, making new connections and relationships is vital if you want your career to move forward.

Second, you need to widen your inter-personal horizons. When you are making work connections, you are not necessarily making friends. The people you work with are often very different from the people you are used to socializing with. They could be from a different generation, or even a different cultural group. But that does not mean that you should avoid the challenge of developing a meaningful and mutually beneficial relationship with these individuals.

Third, keep in mind that social networks are defined as "mutually reciprocal relationships":

People with the best Social Presence understand that networking is as much about being generous – a "go giver" – as it is about being a "go-getter".

Simply translated, this means having an attitude of "What can I do For You?" rather than "What can You Do for Me?" You are much more likely to develop important contacts and career connections if you can show people that you are not always "on the take".

You will be pleasantly surprised by the results when you make it clear to people that you do not expect favors from them. Rather, what you are seeking is to give and receive time, advice, and guidance.

You may wonder what exactly you are in a position to give, particularly if you are in the early stages of your career. Giving can come in many forms, and when you recognize someone's achievements and then ask for their advice, you are giving respect and acknowledgement.

MAKE THE CONNECTIONS

It is important to expose yourself to as many different environments as possible where opportunities exist to connect. So yes, this means you would do well to take advantage of all of those work-related social events that come your way. Another approach is to join a group or association that is relevant to your area of interest.

Example: If you are in sales and marketing, you could join the American Marketing Association. Chances are there will be an active group close to where you live, as well as one online.

Volunteer at every opportunity both in your home and work environment – it will get you visibility very quickly. Joining a social group for tennis/softball or church can prove equally useful. It is also critical to think as broadly as possible. There is no one way to gain access to those important individuals who can help further your career.

Also remember that our Social Presence is not only reserved for people who we perceive as higher ups, or influencers. Every relationship we have with every colleague defines us and contributes to our Social Presence. Now, we are not saying that navigating or networking up is not important; it is, but never overlook your colleagues. Often it is our workmates and con-temporaries, and not the so-called higher ups, who are most influential in our careers.

With that in mind, think about the relationship you have with each and every person you work with every day.

- Do you know what their biggest challenge is?

- Do you ever offer to get them a cup of coffee, or suggest going out for lunch together to work on developing a broader view of the company?

If you come across an opportunity that you think would be appropriate for a colleague, make a point of sharing the information. We guarantee that if you go out of your way to be a resource to your colleagues, you will find that in most cases your generosity will be repaid many times over.

Now that Kat is running a company, one of the things she knows has contributed to her success are the connections she made through industry associations and volunteer groups. In fact, the path leading to her current role was formed through a combination of volunteering for committee work in groups like the Women's Food Service Forum and State Restaurant Associations, and regional franchise groups.

The perspectives she gained and the relationships she built outside her organization helped her learn about opportunities that existed beyond her organization and also taught her ways to be more effective in her job. Through the connections she made, and the subsequent projects she worked on, Kat became both a better employee for her organization and a more developed leader to be qualified for future positions and professional opportunities.

In fact, it was Kat's commitment to building connections that led to her and Nadia's collaboration. Kat volunteered to lead the Membership Committee for the Women's Food Service Forum, and met many leaders of other companies in the food service industry. This in turn led to an invitation to speak on a panel on leadership in the food service industry where Kat, who was a vice president at the time, spoke on a panel with other presidents of large organizations.

The panel was moderated by Nadia, who approached Kat after the event both to compliment her on her presentation, and with an offer to collaborate and do business together. Kat, who didn't know who Nadia was at the time, complimented her right back.

Next, we did what very few people do: Set a date and followed up and had coffee. We recognized that we had many personal and professional similarities and decided to take steps to work together. And that began a relationship of presenting together, providing mutually beneficial opportunities to each other to advance our careers, and building a solid friendship.

Had Kat not volunteered, she would not have found this opportunity. If Nadia had not had the comfort and confidence to approach her to build the connection, we would have missed out on the opportunities to support each other, and we wouldn't have written this book. Those two things together led us to where we are today.

START A CONVERSATION

While the ability to connect is critical to the networking process, it is your skill at meaningful conversation that often solidifies the relationship. Although the prospect may be terrifying, starting a conversation anywhere at any time is much easier than you may think. This does not mean you have to speak to everyone you ever meet, but that after reading this, you will at least know how.

You can start a conversation with a comment on anything from the decor of the room, to the accident you witnessed on your way in, to a compliment on an item such as the pin the person is wearing. In most cases, unless they are extremely busy or distracted, the other party will respond, and thus a conversation begins.

HOW DO YOU KEEP THAT CONVERSATION GOING?

Follow the advice of Dale Carnegie. He characterized people who talk about themselves as "bores", people who talk about others as "gossips", and people who talk about you as "brilliant conversationalists"! If you are at a loss for something to talk about, keep in mind that people are happy to talk about themselves. You can start the ball rolling by asking them about the various phases of their lives: their past, present, and future. You can always ask someone where he or she went to school, or when they first knew they were interested in a particular career.

Current questions can include simply asking what their greatest challenges are, and what they like most/least about their job. When asking about a person's future, good questions can be anything from their plans for their next vacation to their career aspirations.

The biggest mistake people make in attempting to build relationships with people they perceive to have more power than themselves, is going into the meeting with a sense of neediness. Rather, walk into the encounter with a sense of equality. Of course it helps if you do your homework first, so that you are familiar with some recent developments involving their company or career.

Example: You can ask about the challenges facing their company, or make an observation that you have noticed their company's expansion into a particular area. Or, if you are focusing on a particular person, you could compliment him or her on a recent promotion, or a project you are aware of they are working on.

MAKING THE MOST OF A NETWORKING EVENT

Within the realm of starting a conversation, one of the biggest challenges we have all faced at some time is attending a gathering that is filled with strangers. Attending cocktail parties, networking events, or any other interactions can be a great cause of discomfort for some people. If you are one of those people who would rather go for a root canal than attend a networking event, here are some pointers that can make the process a lot less painless – and much more productive.

Start by acknowledging that most people feel just the same way you do. Social unease and discomfort in these situations is universal. However, if you take the role of the initiator, effectively of acting like the host instead of a guest, you will be amazed at the reaction.

You are not a three-year-old in a playground waiting for somebody to ask you to join in a game; neither are you a 16-year-old waiting to be asked to dance.

Be the initiator: Shift from nervous guest to confident host. By this we mean if you are standing next to two individuals, ask them if they know each other. Introduce them to each other and initiate a conversation based on their purpose for attending the event, where in the city they live, what work they do. Once you go from guest passive mode, and from waiting for somebody to talk to you, into the active engager mode, you have more control of the scenario. Like everything else, this takes practice.

Example: This was the case with Gary S., one of our clients, who found attending his wife's business outings particularly daunting. Gary felt like an outsider, always contending with awkward silences and people he perceived to be unfriendly. After attending our program, he went to a company picnic, and tried a new approach.

Instead of waiting for people to approach him, he initiated conversations and made a point of including others. He found his experience was much more pleasant and rewarding. In fact, he made a new golfing buddy, and added several valuable clients.

What happens if you initiate a conversation with someone and it appears they don't want to talk to you? If a group of people you're trying to join doesn't seem to want an additional member, just move on and try someone else. Don't take it personally. They may simply be a group of friends who are more interested in catching up with each other than meeting new people at the moment. One of the biggest mistakes people make at networking events is to persist in trying to interact when it is clear the best course of action is to let it go and move on.

If you are really anxious to make contact with one member of a particular group who does not appear to be open, wait until he or she has left the group, or until you sense from their body language that the group is open to "new members."

How can you tell? You don't want to stare, but you can make some discrete observations, such as noticing whether the group has physically opened up. Have people moved apart? Do the members of this group appear to have turned their attention away from each other? Is there a lull in the conversation and laughter? If you happen to be nearby, perhaps they will actually invite you to join. If not, you can always use the "I couldn't happen but overhear ..." line. It's a cliché, yes, but its intent is easily recognizable and will signal your interest in weighing in on that particular topic.

If you can't seem to break into groups, it is perfectly permissible to approach people who are standing alone. This may, in fact, be the preferred technique if you need to speak with someone in particular. You will then have his or her full attention.

Don't overstay your welcome in a conversation. Once you have accomplished what you need to, like getting an appointment or making an introduction, you can leave.

Don't bail out abruptly, of course; rather, ease your way out, or excuse yourself politely and move on. Once awkward pauses start cropping up in a conversation, it is generally time to move on.

The goal of these events is to make contact with many people, and you won't reach your goal if you glue yourself to someone's side, or allow anyone to glue him- or herself to yours.

The key is to not feel rejected when someone signals that they are ready to move on to another person, or if they don't seem to want to let you into their group.

Keep in mind that everybody has the same goals as you. Use the event as an opportunity to try out conversation tactics and networking advice. That doesn't mean you won't enjoy yourself once you relax and begin to develop confidence.

The final thing you should remember when you are at a networking event is to be as genuine as possible. People can spot a fake. If you're trying to pretend that you're talking to someone because you are enchanted by them, and not because you're there looking for clients, or practicing your networking skills like everyone else, then you will come off as insincere. Be honest that you are attending this event because you want to get something out of it. You are there to meet people who may be in a position to help you further your goals, not necessarily to make lifelong friends (although once in a while it can happen). That's primarily what these events are for, and everybody who is at an event like this pretty much has the same goal.

BECOME A COLLABORATOR

Once you have made those all-important connections, the next step is to incorporate your new contacts into your network. This will not happen by itself: The essence of sustained networking lies in collaboration and on an ongoing attitude of mutual reciprocity. If you want to connect or stay in touch with people you have to work at it. It doesn't happen magically. Maintaining relationships requires specific, sustained effort, and the more thoughtful you can be, the more memorable you will be.

Always exchange contact information or business cards and follow up. Start and maintain a database of the contacts in your network that includes their name, e-mail address, phone number, as well as how, when, and where you met. Include any other pertinent notes to help jar both your memory as well as that of your new contact. Continue adding to this database and make a point of keeping in touch.

Example: If during your conversation you picked up a person's particular area of interest, think about sending him or her a pertinent article or a book suggestion. But be judicious about this. Do not deluge your new contact with "cute stuff" forwarded to you by someone else. And the next time you hear of a spectacular career move by an executive you want to impress, send him or her a congratulatory note on reaching the next phase of an extraordinary career.

TARGETED NETWORKING

At times it can be a challenge to gain access to the executives who actually make the hiring and spending decisions. Many people find this intimidating, but there is no need for you to fall into that category. This is where you need to apply the tools of Targeted Networking.

The first step in this process is to identify the individual or individuals with whom you need to connect. This may sound obvious, but we have often found that people neglect to identify the key players who can help them make a career move or a business connection, even in cases when it involves another department in the same company. Once you do know whom it is you want to reach, then you can develop the most effective approach to gain access.

This strategy might require some lateral thinking.

Example: You would like to be hired by a particular large company to present training programs. Your first thought might be to find a way to meet the CEO. But the more appropriate person to speak to would be the head of Human Resources or Training. Then, using the Internet, it should be easy enough to identify the head of Human Resources. Now, you can simply call her number and speak to her assistant, which could possibly get you a meeting.

A far more efficient approach would be to find out who in your existing network knows him or her. Using that tactic, you might very well find out that you are already connected to several people who work for HR within the company. This is where your Social Presence and networking expertise come in. You can contact these various people, and ask their advice and guidance on the best way to set up a meeting. This approach is far more likely to be successful.

Remember: never demand an introduction; a request will be much more effective.

Example: You could say the following: *"Marvin, you have been so successful in navigating your career at Company X. I would really like to meet with your head of HR. Do you have any advice on the best way to proceed?"*

If you played your cards right, Marvin will volunteer an introduction, which means you already have the advantage.

However, you cannot be sure of or expect such an introduction. These kinds of introductions are a privilege, not a right, and if you take an arrogant approach with your contact, your chances of success will be diminished. In addition, always make a point of thanking the person who is advising you in a way that validates their contribution. This way, they will feel good about helping you out, and they will also benefit from the good vibes your excellent services to Company X will deliver!

The *small Changes* you can make to fine-tune your networking skills are:

- Recognize that your Social Presence is vital for successful networking.

- Widen your interpersonal horizons to include your coworkers as well as those higher up.

- Become a "go giver", and signal your willingness to collaborate rather than compete.

- Work on staying in touch.

The *BIG IMPACT*: You will move beyond simply making connections into developing rewarding relationships.

CHAPTER 6

SOCIAL MEDIA AS A NETWORKING TOOL

We live in an era of rapid change that has been driven by dramatic advances in technology, particularly as it relates to how we communicate and do business. In this kind of environment, standing still or hiding in your cubicle and "just doing your job" is not an option. The world will pass you by before you know it. We have found that you can strongly enhance your overall presence and brand by staying current. Whether it is how you dress, staying up-to-date on current affairs, or leveraging updated technology to elevate your Virtual Presence, simply staying current is one of the top ways to make a *BIG IMPACT* on everything you do.

We define Virtual Presence as the enhancement of your Personal Brand through writing, phone, e-mail, and social media. Your presence in cyberspace is as much a reflection of your overall brand as your physical, interpersonal, and social presence – and it is one of those areas where making *small Changes* can truly have a *BIG IMPACT*.

This doesn't mean you need to jump on each and every social media development that comes by. You don't need to immerse yourself in social media or e-mail to the extent it detracts from your job, but you do need to be aware of how these tools can help build your reputation and connections that become your community.

Whether you are aware of it or not, you probably have a Virtual Presence already on the Internet.

- Have you checked yours lately?

- Do you have a complete LinkedIn profile that positively reflects all of your achievements?

- Or is your online presence dominated by pictures on Facebook that show you partying with a drink in hand?

One way is to Google yourself; in fact, in all our workshops we suggest that participants Google themselves at least once every few months. You will likely be surprised to discover what comes up. For many of us, it can range from donations to organizations that you support, to listings in alumni organizations, and professional ratings that you didn't even know you had received. You may even find that someone has posted and tagged you in an ancient beach or kindergarten photograph, or a staff party from three jobs ago! The key point is you need to be able to control what you want a prospective employer, or an HR professional, or colleague in your company to see.

There are as many ways enhance your overall Virtual Presence and impact as there are to sabotage it. Most of us are very aware of the awesome potential to swiftly derail a career via cyberspace. We have seen prominent politicians and sports stars crash and burn over inappropriate e-mails or Twitter posts, and successful people lose good jobs because they succumbed to the often irresistible urge to express themselves via a Facebook post, a Twitter Tweet, or an e-mail rant that somehow went public. It is also possible to miss both personal and professional opportunities due to a less-than-appealing Virtual Presence.

Whether it's the inevitable "e-mail wars" that ensue in a corporate environment, having unflattering or inappropriate photos or content online, or missing opportunities to leverage other forms of virtual connection and communication, there is much to learn and master.

Given the wide range of information available on the Internet, it can be difficult to craft your own Virtual Presence. In fact, a mini industry has sprung up with names like Reputation Defender whose sole purpose is to monitor the Internet and "clean up" potentially negative information that has been posted about an individual or company.

While we are not suggesting that you get professional help to craft an online presence, we do recommend a range of measures you can use to ensure that your online presence has the maximum positive impact, and that the material is what you want a potential employer, colleague, or client to see.

Although the vast majority of us feel that we have at least mastered the basics of e-mail and cell phone communications, it can be daunting to take on the rapidly evolving world of cyberspace. It may sometimes seem that you have only just begun to understand and use a particular service – like Twitter or Facebook – when a whole new and potentially important service starts to emerge and evolve. Between this, and the widely publicized examples of promising careers that have tanked as a result of injudicious use of social media, many are tempted to just sit the whole thing out.

While coaching and training in this area, we often hear the response, "Well, I just won't be online." That isn't the solution. Not only will you be missing out on an increasingly important way to enhance your professional presence, but frankly, you probably already have an online presence. And in fact, as technology advances, it is more likely that others may encounter you online before they do in person. Sites like YouTube, Google, Flickr, Facebook, Pinterest, and many more allow easy access and a sneak peak at your life. You are being branded whether or not you are consciously involved in the process!

It is also vital to exploit the opportunity that a cyber presence offers. Businesses, communities, families, and groups are living their lives online. Despite its potential perils, having a Virtual Presence is a wonderful opportunity to connect, find others, and be found.

According to a recent report from the website, Jobvite, a significant majority of employers are using social media to find new hires. Therefore, don't hide. Set out to learn about the most important social media platforms so you can build a Virtual Presence with intention while always being fully aware of the associated networking tools and pitfalls.

We must emphasize, as does social networking expert Denise Evens Elsbree, "You need to take this seriously, and take the time to do it right."

LINKING IN

Experts in the field believe that the first place to create and consolidate your Virtual Presence is to join LinkedIn. With over 44 million users in the United States – and over 100 million worldwide – LinkedIn is geared toward making professional as opposed to social connections. LinkedIn users are able to build a professional network by posting a profile which serves as an online resume, that can facilitate your ability to make profitable connections. Many search engines are optimized to come to LinkedIn first. Having a solid LinkedIn presence not only provides a solid base for your online presence; it can also help to displace potentially negative information about you.

Here are some of the small steps you can take to **Maximize your LinkedIn Impact**:

- Post a complete profile, and enhance it with a professional quality photograph.

- As a corollary, keep in mind that an incomplete or sketchy LinkedIn profile will detract from your Virtual Presence.

- Give an accurate account of your past employment.

- Fill out sections on links, books, and blogs. This helps tell the world about your professional interests – it makes you more than just another profile online.

- When you invite others to connect with you here, be sure to use a customized invitation with a lead-in of a personal note that shows why you want to connect with that person.

- Recommend others you have worked with. It's a great way to generate LinkedIn activity, and it's possible they may recommend you right back.

- Use groups to connect with other professionals and elevate your overall profile.

- Look through LinkedIn and find people you admire, as well as others in your position and industry, to get great, real world examples of phrases and descriptions to use on your LinkedIn page.

Remember: What you are creating on LinkedIn is a well thought-out living resume that is even more powerful because you are crafting a portrait of yourself through your links, details, and other features that clearly answer the question, "Who is this person... really?"

USING FACEBOOK FOR MORE THAN "JUST FRIENDS"

Facebook is another excellent way to stay connected. Many people have the attitude that Facebook is intended for strictly personal interaction.

In fact, social networking expert, Denise Evans Elsbree, has likened Facebook to a "cocktail party". Denise says, "It's supposed to be fun!"

Facebook *is* fun, and a great way to easily share photographs and stay connected with the people in your life, particularly if you have a network that is spread all over the country and overseas. Understandably, most people feel they are entitled to personal privacy that should extend to personal online communication. In fact, one of the most common rebuttals we hear is, "My personal life is personal and my professional life is professional – and I want them kept separate."

If this is how you feel, you are not alone. But you can control how you link the various elements of your social media presence online. How you present yourself online is always a personal choice, and how available you make yourself, both personally and professionally is typically driven by many personal factors. We have seen many perspectives on this, and none are wrong, but if you are trying to maximize your Virtual Presence and to be found by all the opportunities out there, the math is more in your favor if you have productive, positive profiles in multiple places.

In addition, businesses and organizations are also using Facebook, and the more available you are, the more real, believable, and approachable your profiles appear to be. Even if you limit Facebook to your personal life, be aware that, privacy measures notwithstanding, chances are your professional contacts, be they supervisors or potential employers, could come across your Facebook profile. The extent to which employers can use questionable Facebook negative posts as grounds for demoting or terminating an employee is already becoming a hot legal issue.

With that in mind, here are some *small Changes* you can make that will maximize your Facebook impact and lessen the chance of a Facebook disaster:

- If you are concerned about your privacy, it is important to regularly review your Security Settings, not the least because Facebook is known to frequently make internal changes, and sometimes without notification.

- The Security Settings will affect who can see your information, your posts, and the posts of others on your wall. You can make your profile and your wall as public or private as you'd like, but be aware that many experts warn users that these Security Settings can be unreliable. As one HR professional pointed out, "If anybody has a camera, behave. You can control what you do, but you can't control what others put up."

- If you are having a bad day at work, resist the urge to tell the world about it on your Facebook status.

- By the same token, and for the same reason, don't "vent" on Facebook, unless you are very sure that this is an opinion you want to share with friends and possibly many others. Remember, if a friend "likes" what you say, your thoughts can travel around the world much faster than a speeding bullet!

- Avoid using expletives and juvenile language.

- When you click the "like" button on other pages, groups, and entities, this will reflect who you are as a person. Think carefully about what you want to communicate about yourself to the outside world.

- Be aware that others can "tag" you in photos or posts. Theoretically, Facebook is supposed to notify you when this happens. As long as you keep a watchful eye, you can manage that, but again, take the time to find out how to remove tags, if necessary.

- Check your company's policies or procedures and guidelines on Facebook and other social media sites, and be sure to follow them. People have lost jobs for posting on Facebook when they shouldn't, particularly if they work in a field – like healthcare or education – where confidentiality is required by law.

BLOGS: A CHANCE TO WRITE YOUR OWN STORY

Blogs are websites filled with content and discussions about a topic. If you have the time and really want to establish a rich virtual presence, consider starting a blog of your own. There are millions of blogs out there. Many are personal, and can range from a travelogue to chronicles about someone's pet ferret, to Adventures in Italian Cooking.

Some have a political or social agenda. Others are established by professionals to expand their reach into the marketplace, build relationships, and create influence. The benefit of authoring an effective blog is it puts you in control of shaping your online brand. You can also position yourself as an individual with valuable expertise. There are many examples of blogs that have been started by individuals anxious to express themselves on a particular topic that have evolved into important and lucrative websites.

Example: Three blogs that Kat turns to regularly are...

- sethgodin.com, developed by Seth Godin, who is considered an authority on marketing;

- Gary Vaynershuk, who specializes in social media and branding; and

- Keith Ferrazi on building meaningful relationships and connections.

- (*You can also check out Kat's blog at katcole.net, and Nadia's at nadiaspeaks.com.*)

While all of these blogs have very different content, discussions, and purposes, ultimately they all enable their authors to connect with people they would otherwise not connect with. They also provide opportunities to help others through their discussion forums, or to be recognized for projects you are working on. You can learn from people you would otherwise never know, and you can both share and adopt best practices.

There really are no rules about how to write an effective blog, but there are certainly best practices.

What follows are some small tips that can have a *BIG IMPACT* on your blogging presence:

- Templates are available that remove the intimidation and difficulty of starting your own blog. The two most popular are Blogger.com and Wordpress.com, but there are many others.

- Meaningful content is the key to successful blogging. Simply stated, you must have something to say that people want to hear.

- Interact with your readers and discussion forums frequently.

- The best way to improve your blog is read other blogs, and learn from other successful bloggers.

- Be sure to connect your blog with other social media sites such as your LinkedIn, Twitter and Facebook.

- When done properly, blogging and interacting with others can take as little as 15 minutes a day. We know that not everybody has the time to regularly and meaningfully interact; however, if you do have a blog, you need to keep it reasonably current.

- Make a point of carving out some time in your schedule to blog, once, twice, or three times a week.

- Always keep in mind that like any online profile, a blog is a representation of who you are, and it becomes part of the online content that is discovered when someone Googles you.

AND IF YOU HAVEN'T TWEETED...

Twitter is a microblogging site. While blogs are web pages where people write personal articles and content, a microblog is essentially the same thing, but much, much smaller. Twitter microblogs, also known as "Tweets", are limited to 140 characters. That doesn't seem like a lot, but 140 characters, carefully crafted, can communicate a lot of important information. There are even people who write Twitter poetry!

Twitter is a wonderful place to:

- Learn from others;

- Filter news, content, and updates based on information you prefer; and

- Connect with others in and out of your industry and immediate community.

Twitter is used by companies to connect with consumers and applicants. It's used by individuals to connect with people all around the globe. And it's used by many organizations for marketing, research, and service. There are literally millions of people online each day seeking connections and content. Because they are searching, if you are there, you are more likely to be found. Similarly, with all the activity on this site, you are likely to have another conduit to communicate with potential connections and employers.

Like other websites that fall under the category of Social Media, Twitter can be intimidating at first. There is so much activity, and most who aren't a part of it typically say, "I just don't get it!" But check out one of the many online Twitter tutorials, both text and video, and you'll quickly become more comfortable with it. You may realize it's just the connecting and branding opportunity you've been looking for.

Twitter is a good complementary site to leverage if you have a website, Facebook page, or a blog. You can tweet content you have on the other sites to reach more people. Twitter can be a megaphone for content you want to share, or updates you think people in your community may want to know. It's just like building community and connections in person: You need to take interest in others before expecting they will take interest in you. But if you remember that community mindset, Twitter can be a resource to take your Virtual Presence to another level.

One way we use Twitter is to reinforce and support our friends, clients, and colleagues. We will often "retweet" something of interest to spread content and to help broadcast the useful and helpful messages of other brands or peers. We also use it as an extension of our approach to networking.

Twitter can be used to find thought leaders on any topic. You can connect to them and build both online and in-person relationships.

Example: Kat was working on a marketing project and needed to find marketing leaders and information. She went to Twitter, used the search function, typed in "marketing research", and found conversations online about her specific topic.

She found thought leaders on the topic and she connected with them through Twitter. She complimented them on their research and perspectives, asked questions, and built a relationship online. These were leaders she would not otherwise have found, or had access to. Through these discoveries and relationships created through Twitter, Kat was able to progress more quickly on her own initiatives. And later she was able to meet these leaders in person, and has continued to work with some of them on various new projects.

DON'T TAKE E-MAIL ETIQUETTE FOR GRANTED!

Most of us have been using personal e-mail for so long, we forget that we need to apply a separate and stricter set of rules to business e-mails.

At this point, e-mail is probably the most important way that we communicate with friends and colleagues. Unfortunately, it is remarkably easy to annoy people and derail friendships (and your career) via a thoughtless electronic missive.

Think about the things that bother you in e-mail. We have found that all of our groups across the country and around the world have the same pet peeves:

- Quick replies that show a lack of awareness.

- E-mails that include cc's that clearly are intended to create fear.

- Setting up an endless round of e-mails by hitting "Reply All", or responding thank you, to the thank you, to the no thank you.

- Misspellings...especially unforgivable with Spell Check available on almost all e-mail platforms.

- A lack of awareness about the tone of an e-mail.

- Emoticons (Smiley faces), text language, and other annoying symbols.

- E-mails that ramble on and on for way too long.

- E-mails with not enough direct information, or that don't reply to your query in a way that you can make sense of the answer.

- E-mail etiquette can be enhanced by simple awareness, not the least of which is the realization that e-mail messages sometimes travel much faster than we think.

Take these small steps that can have a *BIG IMPACT*:

- Always press your mental "pause" button and review what you have written before you hit the "Send" button.

- E-mail with purpose, not out of frustration or anger: If you wouldn't say it face-to-face, it has no place in e-mail.

- Change your subject line with every e-mail. Make it as compelling, brief, and informative as possible.

- Check your intention. As we emphasize in our workshops on presentation skills, be clear about the purpose of your communication and its audience.

- Always have a signature that has your contact information and links to relevant social media sites to be sure recipients always know how and where to contact you in addition to "Reply". However, keep your e-mail signature simple so that it does not clog up your e-mail, or get caught in a spam filter.

• Do not re-forward cute articles, jokes, and animated gags that were forwarded to you, especially if they are in the form of an attachment. Often these attachments contain viruses. There is probably no worse way to sabotage a business relation-ship than to accidentally send someone a virus that disables, takes over, or crashes their computer.

Use these small ways to avoid the BIG and all-too-common e-mail wars that can cripple careers and reputations:

Be the one mature individual who stops the e-mail chain! Stop the madness. Actually pick up the phone and call that person – or even better, go see them if you can. It's amazing how the intensity and stress is instantly lowered when people have to communicate face-to-face or over the phone.

We are all for technology – who doesn't have a special relationship with their Smartphones? But we have learned the hard way how reacting to disagreements with snappy e-mails can be destructive, both personally and professionally. In addition to our own major e-mail mistakes, we've seen everyone from entry level assistants to high powered executives make themselves look petty and powerless by getting caught up in the defensive and "CYA" (cover your ass) e-mail wars. Don't do it! Stand out by speaking up in person!

We frequently recommend some of these small measures that can have a *BIG IMPACT* on your e-mail presence:

- Take the e-mail bar containing "Send" out of your viewed toolbar. It makes you have to take one extra step to go to "File" then "Send" – but it prevents the accidental send.

- Assume that whoever reads your e-mail thinks you are in a bad mood, or that you don't like them, then read it with that "lens". Now, rewrite it so that person only gets the important message you intend to send. E-mail has no tone of its own. It takes on the attitude that the recipient assumes the sender has – which often is less positive than the sender's intentions.

- Beware of getting comfortable with "text talk" with colleagues. If you are the type of person who feels friendly and relaxed with anyone, you may automatically e-mail or text things like: "c u soon" or "lol". Eventually, you will assume others know what you mean. This could lead to a misunderstanding – was it "laugh out loud" or "lots of love"? – which can give the impression to someone that you are unprofessional.

- Turn off auto-correct if you have a habit of typing and sending messages. You'll be surprised what your "smart" phone thinks you are trying to type.

- Save the text-a-bet for friends and family. Make an effort to speak and type in full words to strangers, new acquaintances, and definitely to colleagues, customers, and bosses.

In general, polished writing skills are as reflective of your overall presence as every other type of communication. Make them as much a part of your virtual communication repertoire as they would be on paper.

YOUR SMARTPHONE: YOUR FRIEND AND YOUR ENEMY

Being mobile is an important part of our lives, and Web-enabled smartphones, those multi-functional mini computers that can fit into your front pocket, are the key ingredient. If you think about it, they are truly wondrous devices that not only can carry on a telephone conversation, but can also take pictures, seek out important business information, and locate the best restaurant in town – all at the same time!

In fact, the average smartphone has the kind of computing and communications power that used to fill a whole room in the ancient days of the computer mainframe. It is no surprise that smartphones are immensely popular, with more than 60 million users in the United States alone, a figure that is expected to grow by the tens of millions annually.

However, as useful as they undeniably are, the bewitching quality of our smartphones can blind us to their impact on our overall persona. Seemingly trivial details, such as their enormous potential for entertainment and distraction, as well as your choice of ringtone, your addiction to texting, and other common errors due to being in a hurry or on-the-go, can detract from your overall presence.

Remember: You build the perception of your Personal Brand moment by moment, through every small interaction – both verbal and nonverbal. You cannot choose which interactions people remember, but you can choose how and when you have the interaction. Be sensitive to the fact that even though a majority of your friends and peers have smartphones, using it, looking at it, or even having it visible in certain scenarios can be regarded as unprofessional, or worse, rude.

Once the moment, phone call, e-mail, texting, or encounter has passed, it's done – and it has become a part of others' perception of you. If you are self-aware, you know when you are in a place where you shouldn't text, make, or answer a call.

Equally important, make a point of never conducting private conversations in public. You may think you can hold an interpersonal conversation and text at the same time, but be assured that the only person you are fooling is yourself.

So it follows: thoughtfully manage these small interactions, whether they are in person, online, or on the phone, to make a *BIG IMPACT* on how you're perceived.

- Feel free to have the latest hip-hop or dance song as your ring tone, but when in a professional setting, have it on silent or vibrate. You can show individuality with your devices, but there is certainly a time and place for funny songs and symbols.

- On a scale of 1-10, how would you rate your telephone answering voice?

  o Have you ever even thought of it?

  o Does it project enthusiasm, energy, and professionalism?

  o Or do you sound tired, bored, or distracted?

  o How you answer matters. It is a reflection of who you are.

    If you feel you are going to sound distracted, let it go to voicemail, where the caller should find a strong, confident, concise mailbox greeting.

    If you put yourself in the position of answering when you are rushed or already frustrated, it's likely the caller

> *will misunderstand your tone to be reflective of how you feel about them.*

- Remember to acknowledge receipt; when a note comes across, you may feel compelled to send a full thoughtful reply, but don't have the time to do so. Send a quick note saying, "Thanks, will reply soon" or "I'm on the road, and I'll call you on this shortly." This ensures you look responsive, but still gives you the time you need to respond fully and appropriately.

- If you don't have access to a spell-checker on your device, and you're not sure if you've typed a word correctly, switch to a word that you do know the spelling and say the same thing with different words.

PUTTING IT ALL IN WRITING ...

On the topic of written communications, be aware that how you write reflects on you. Poor spelling and grammar can quickly spoil a professional image.

Writing coach Leslie Ayres makes the point that even if you weren't hired to write for a living, writing well – whether in e-mails, PowerPoint presentations or memos – is an important element of every job.

Here are some common grammatical and spelling errors to avoid:

- Confusing possessive pronouns with contractions:

- o You're means you are.

- o Who's is short for who is, and

- o it's is short for it is.

Even though we use an apostrophe to denote possession in the case of nouns, like the dog's bone, we do not use an apostrophe in the case of a possessive pronoun. That coat is *yours*; the dog hurt *its* paw; and it is often not clear *whose* cell phone went off in the middle of a meeting.

- There is no such word as alot:

  Kat likes to drink *a lot* of coffee, and our children expect us to *allot* – or share out – favors fairly.

- Every day is usually two words; it is only one word when used as an adjective to describe a noun:

  We go to work *every day*, and getting caught in traffic is an *everyday* experience in big cities like Atlanta!

- Beware of writing in sentence fragments, even though our conversations are full of them.

  "Because I said so!" is something your mother might say, but don't start a sentence with words like because, since, when, whenever, while, and as, without completing the thought, as in *Since the weather has changed, I have started wearing closed shoes to work.*

- It is equally important to recognize and avoid run-on sentences and comma splices:

  These happen when you try to join together groups of words that could be sentences on their own with a comma. *Writing well is an important skill, it helps enhance your professional presence* is incorrect. Rather, write the following: *Writing well is an important skill, for it helps enhance your professional presence,* or *Writing well is an important skill because it helps enhance your professional presence.*

- Observe subject-verb agreement:

  The staff members *are* meeting, but the staff *is* meeting.

- If you need to write a longer memo, it is always a good idea to make sure that you have clearly communicated your point of view.

- Also, follow the rule of developing a good paragraph:

  Limit each paragraph to one main idea and its supporting details.

Most word processing programs have spell check and the capacity to highlight grammatical and spelling errors and suggest changes, but these systems are not infallible.

It never hurts to be aware of these and other common errors without resorting to the program. There are also numerous websites that can give you grammar and composition pointers, and help you enhance your vocabulary. Two very useful websites are the Purdue University Online Writing Laboratory, and the Online Writing Laboratory sponsored by Towson University in Maryland.

Remember to use the tips in this chapter not only to enhance your Personal Brand and connect with others virtually, but also to be sure you are not detracting from your reputation.

The **small Changes** to enhance your Virtual Presence are:

- Take the time to educate yourself about social media.

- Be conscious that anything you post online contributes to your brand.

- Press the mental "pause" button before you send anything; reflect, rethink, retype, then send.

- Be aware of smartphone abuse, particularly in the company of others.

The **BIG IMPACT** will be a strong Virtual Presence which is an immensely powerful way for you to remain current, enhance your Personal Brand, and develop new connections.

CHAPTER 7

TIME FOR TRANSFORMATION

We wrote this book for all of you. Those who feel stuck in place at work, spinning your wheels while your other equally or perhaps even lesser qualified colleagues have moved ahead. And for those who are looking to turbo charge an already successful career. We have shared our secrets. These are not mammoth transformations. Rather, they are small, incremental changes anyone can make that will have a *BIG IMPACT* on maximizing your presence, opening opportunities in life, and accelerating your career. In fact, we have seen participants in our workshops and presentations transform themselves, their careers, and their prospects after just one session.

There are no mysteries or magic. Instead we have shared concrete steps you can take to accomplish the following:

- Leverage the power of your Personal Brand by cultivating self-awareness, practicing accountability, and always projecting a "What can I do for you?" attitude.

- Enhance your physical presence by being conscious of the impact of your appearance and carrying yourself like a professional.

- Develop interpersonal skills that defuse conflicts and enhance your ability to interact with others.

- Cultivate and expand meaningful relation-ships inside and outside of your company and industry, and increase your ability to network and gain access.

- Harness the growing power of Social Media to build your professional network and enhance your brand.

NOW, IT'S JUST ABOUT DOING IT!

Start with a quick personal inventory:
What do you need to:

1. **Stop doing?**

2. **Start doing?**

3. **Continue doing?**

What are the *small Changes* you can make? It could be anything from purchasing a tailored jacket, to resolving to assume positive intent with an important colleague, to updating your LinkedIn profile.

Decide on your personal first small step and take action! When you walk into your next meeting you have tomorrow morning, be aware of the way you are communicating both verbally and nonverbally in each interaction. It is important not to overthink what you are doing. Just be aware that your identity and Personal Brand are not set in stone, but people form an impression of you moment by moment, interaction by interaction, and you have a chance to make an impact on that every day.

Your transformation doesn't just end with reading our book; it is an ongoing journey. Remember that enhancing your Presence and leveraging the power of your Personal Brand is not a secret process; all we have done is given things a name and decoded their elements. Look around and you will see examples everywhere of individuals who are successful at enhancing their Personal Brand – and others whose attitude and physical presence are barriers to their success. Keep an eye out for the people who are most influential around you and identify the characteristics that they possess. Identify the elements of Professional Presence in action, and emulate their behaviors yourself.

Our gift to you through this book is enhanced self-awareness that will give you a significant advantage in your chosen career, and your life. Now it's time for you to focus and take action.

Begin the journey. Don't put it off till next month, or even next week. Begin it now.

Stephen Covey refers to most of our daily activity as the "whirlwind." He argues that to become truly productive, we need to focus on being strategic and not let the 'whirlwind' distract us. Sometimes that first step is the hardest; we all have so much going on in our lives that we can find it hard to focus. But you can do it: Start with one thing you would like to do differently over the coming year, and focus your energy, time, and resources on making it happen.

We are not looking at gargantuan, over-whelming measures. We are suggesting incre-mental changes that can make every interaction, every presentation, every tweet, and every post an opportunity to enhance your overall presence. And most important, enjoy the process.

Have fun making *small changes* that will give you a *BIG IMPACT* in your world.

ACKNOWLEDGEMENTS & DEDICATIONS

Nadia Bilchik: You have no idea how happy we are that you are reading our book about the *small Changes* that can have the *BIGGEST IMPACT.*

We started writing this book shortly after we met in 2006, and like it always does, LIFE got in the way, so the biggest thanks goes to our editor, Miriam Lacob Stix for her endless patience, wonderful writing and editing, and most importantly for never losing either her temper or our files. We often heard her say that trying to get two overcommitted women to write a book is like catching water with a fishing net. So, Mir, thanks again for the midnight chats and your ability to interpret two women who speak as fast as their minds work.

Gratitude also to Cliff Carle, our publishing consultant and editor's editor. You had the nicest way of telling us when our writing needed more of the oomph we have in our presentations. Thanks also for telling us that lots of red on our manuscript isn't as depressing as we might think at first. You gave us both hope and help!

A huge thanks to the Coca-Cola company for hosting a Women's Food Service panel, where we both spoke and met for the first time. A fortuitous meeting indeed!

And we love Ted Turner, not only for CNN, but for hosting the Georgia Restaurant Association Gala in 2006 where we realized how well we worked together, and where we met the lovely Elizabeth Dewberry.

To every person we have ever coached, or audience we have ever been in front of, from Home Depot to Turner Entertainment Networks, from CNN to Kaiser-Permanente, Coca-Cola, Morgan Stanley Smith Barney, Porsche, SAKS, and ESPN: Thank you for the privilege. Thank you for providing us with endless stories and insights. We learn from you as much as you from us.

Other amazing, inspiring people we want to thank who have helped us along our respective journeys in ways too numerous to mention are Daphne Schechter of Schechter Consulting, Jeff Halter of YWomen, Nancy Neill, ACG, Suzanne Hanein, Everyday Gourmet, Denise Elsbree and Ron Slotin, Trio Media Group, Tonya Thomas, Koos Bekker, MNET TV, South Africa, T.J. Holmes, BET, Tenisha Bell, CNN, Mike Daugherty, LabMD, Dr. Joy, Carver and Associates, and all the wonderful people who have been instrumental in navigating this journey.

To the amazing Kat Cole my friend, partner and colleague: Your humility and brilliance continue to inspire me.

Finally, I dedicate this book to my husband, Steve, for all the BIG and small things you do, and to my daughters Alexa and Julia who continue to have the BIGGEST IMPACT.

Kat Cole: To my partner, Chris Wagner – one of the funniest, smartest and most supportive people I know. You never stopped supporting the work on this book, four years in the making, all while I was going back to school, going through the sale of a company, changing jobs and maintaining a schedule with constant travel. I have to say I will not miss hearing, "Aren't you done yet?"

To my family: the woman who taught me to go after every opportunity – Jo Barsh, my incredibly resilient mother, her husband, Jerry Barsh who became a great father to my sisters and me, my sisters Cherie and Gina and their kids Ethan, Kendal, and Alyssa. I hope this book makes you proud and has a few tidbits you can share with others as you impact your communities.

To the Women's Foodservice Forum for providing content, experiences, and connections that have been a staple in my professional development for almost a decade. To Georgia State University's incredible Executive MBA program, J. Mack Robinson School of Business faculty, cohorts, and resources. I am proud to be a Panther!

To the women at My Sister's House, Weaver House, and Partners Against Domestic Violence in Atlanta, and all those who are served by organizations that help lift families out of abuse and poverty: I hope this book provides more tools in your toolbox to help you get that job or promotion you want, and maximize opportunities for you and your family as you transition from tough times to triumph.

To the extremely talented writer and dear friend Elizabeth Dewberry; to all the leaders who volunteer their time to those in need in our communities; to Neville Isdell for sharing the message of Connected Capitalism, and helping businesses large and small understand how to connect business to society.

To Nadia – you are a great wife, mother, and friend; and you are so truly gifted at what you do. Your ability to help individuals elevate their presence to have greater impact is nothing short of amazing. Whether you are on camera at CNN, or in front of thousands of employees of international corporations, your speaking, teaching, and coaching ability are world class. It is beautiful to watch someone live their purpose through their work.

While I could list an entire book of names, I must acknowledge these people as influencers in my life: To the organizations and people who have supported and inspired me over the years: Women's Foodservice Forum Board of Directors, Staff and Volunteers, National Restaurant Association, Georgia Restaurant Association, Alice Elliot, Phil Hickey, leaders and teams at Roark Capital, FOCUS Brands, and Cinnabon, Inc., Sanofi Aventis, Firm of Arnall, Golden & Gregory, Georgia State University, J. Mack Robinson College of Business. All the leaders and employees of Hooters Restaurants worldwide, Council of Hotel and Restaurant Trainers, my fellow Changers of Commerce: Amanda Hite, Jim Knight, Brandon and Katy Hill, Nicole Walls, Joni and Wally Doolin; all the cool people I get to connect with and learn from on Twitter, Facebook, YouTube and in the Blogosphere. To all those who over the years have said, "You should write a book." Thanks for the encouragement and support – this one's for you!

BIBLIOGRAPHY

Tony Allessandro (2000) *Charisma: Seven Keys to Developing the Magnetism That Leads Success.* Warner Books, Inc.

Jack L. Canfield, Mark Victor Hansen, Maida Rogerson, Martin Rutte & Tim Clauss (2001) *Chicken Soup for the Soul at Work.* Health Communications, Inc.

Dale Carnegie & Arthur Pell, Ed. (1990) *How to Win Friends and Influence People.* Simon and Schuster Adult Publishing Group.

Robert B. Cialdini (2008) *Influence: Science and Practice.* 5th Edition. Prentice Hall.

Harvey J. Coleman (2010) *Empowering Yourself: The Organizational Game Revealed.* Authorhouse.

Stephen Covey (2004) *The Seven Habits of Highly Effective People.* Free Press.

David D'Allessandro (2008) *Career Warfare: 10 Rules for Building Your Successful Brand on the Business Battlefield.* McGraw-Hill.

Keith Ferrazzi & Tahl Raz (2005) *Never Eat Alone: And Other Secrets to Success, One Relationship at a Time.* Doubleday Publishing.

Rick Frishman, Jill Lublin & Mark Steisel (2004) *Networking Magic: Find the Best – from Doctors,*

Lawyers, and Accountants, to Homes, Schools and Jobs. Adams Media Corporation.

Ken Futch (2005) *Take Your Best Shot: Turning Situations Into Opportunities*. Wagrub Press.

Malcolm Gladwell (2002) *The Tipping Point: How Little Things Can Make a Big Difference*. Back Bay Books.

Seth Godin – sethgodin.com

Marshall Goldsmith (2007) *What Got You Here Won't Get You There: How Successful People Become Even More Successful*. Hyperion.

Daniel Goleman (2002) *Working with Emotional Intelligence*. Bantam Books.

Daniel Goleman (2005) *Emotional Intelligence*. Bantam Books.

Mark Goulson (1996) *Get Out of Your Own Way: Overcoming Self-defeating Behavior*. Perigee Trade.

Mark Goulson (2009) *Just Listen: Discover the Secret to Getting Through to Absolutely Anyone*. AMACOM

Jason Jennings (2012) *Think Big. Act Small. How America's Best Companies Keep the Start-up Spirit Alive*. Penguin USA.

John Kehoe (1997) *Mind Power into the 21st Century. Techniques for Success and Happiness*. Zoetic Books.

Douglas T. Kenrick, Ed. (2012) *Influence: Science, Application and the Psychology of Robert Cialdini*. Oxford.

Robert S. Littell & Donna Fisher (2001) *Power Netweaving: 10 Secrets to Successful Relationship Marketing*. National Underwriting Company.

Harvey B. Mackay (1999) *Dig Your Well Before You're Thirsty: The Only Networking Book You'll Ever Need*. Doubleday Publishing.

Harvey B. Mackay (2005) *Swim with the Sharks Without Being Eaten Alive.* HarperCollins Publishers.

William Marston (1999; originally published 1928) *Emotions of Normal People.* Taylor & Francis Ltd.

Albert Mehrabian (2007) *Nonverbal Communication.* Transaction Publishers.

Barbara Pease (2006) *The Definitive Book of Body Language.* Random House Publishing Group.

Susan RoAne (2000) *How to Work a Room: The Ultimate Guide to Savvy Socializing in Person and Online.* HarperCollins Publishers.

Anthony Robbins, Joseph McClendon, & Dominick V. Anfuso (2006) *Inner Strength: Harnessing the Power of Your Six Primal Needs.* Free Press.

Anthony Robbins (1992) *Awaken the Giant Within: How to Take Immediate Control of Your Mental, Emotional, Physical and Financial Destiny.* Simon and Schuster Adult Publishing Group.

Don Miguel Ruiz (1997) *The Four Agreements.* Amber-Allen Publishing.

Richard Stengel (2010) *Mandela's Way. Fifteen Lessons on Life, Love and Courage.* Crown Publishing Group.

Timothy Sharp (2008) *The Happiness Handbook.* Finch Publishing.

Jerry S. Wilson (2008) *Managing Brand You. Seven Steps to Creating Your Most Successful Self.* AMACOM.

Zig Ziglar (2000) *See You at the Top.* Pelican Publishing Company, Inc.

ABOUT THE AUTHORS

Nadia Bilchik, President of Greater Impact Communication, is an internationally renowned television personality, media and communication training expert, author, and keynote speaker. Nadia currently reports for CNN's Weekend Morning Passport, has anchored and hosted feature programs for CNN International, CNN Airport Network and MNet Television (South Africa). Nadia's unique, fun, and practical approach to Maximizing Personal Presence and Leveraging the Power of Your Personal Brand comes from her experience interviewing and consulting with world renowned figures, celebrities, and corporations. These include Richard Gere, George Clooney, Tom Hanks, Meryl Streep, and Anthony Hopkins. She has provided professional development training, consulting, and keynote addresses to many organizations including Turner Broadcasting, Coca-Cola, ESPN, The Home Depot, Delta, Equifax, Accenture, Network of Executive Women (NEW) and Women's Food Service Forum. Nadia has emceed numerous events with renowned individuals such as Nelson Mandela, Ted Turner, and Richard Branson. She is the author of *The Little Book of Big Networking Ideas: A Guide to Expert Networking*. Through her enlightening seminars and keynote speeches she has helped thousands of people to become successful in their careers and personal lives. Nadia graduated from the University of Cape Town and has a Licentiate in Speech and Drama from Trinity College in London.

Kat Cole is President of Cinnabon, Inc. at Focus Brands, and a member of the Board of Directors of the Women's Foodservice Forum. Over the course of just nine years, Kat advanced from her first job in the food service industry to becoming Vice President at Hooters of America, Inc. as well as a sought-after speaker and consultant for a wide range of companies, universities and industry organizations and has won awards ranging from global women of influence and volunteer of the year to Atlanta's 40 Under 40 to watch. She transitioned from executive leadership at Hooters of America, Inc. to become Chief Operating Officer and then President of Cinnabon, Inc., driving growth for the multi-channel brand.

In addition to her involvement in many local and global organizations that help communities and individuals lift themselves out of poverty, Kat travels all over the world as a volunteer and volunteer group leader for organizations that support ending childhood hunger and elevating women. She also works with groups in developing countries that provide skills training, economic development, and sustainable practices.

As a business consultant and executive coach, Kat's many skills include building effective cross cultural and cross-generation teams and relationships, consumer brand building, using strategies of virtual and community connection to grow business, and developing interpersonal skills to manage the implementation of difficult change.

Kat has an MBA from Georgia State University's J. Mack Robinson College of Business.